THE ALICE BAILEY INHERITANCE

An informed commentary on the founder of the Arcane
School who stated she drew her inspiration and knowledge
from inner plane 'Masters'.

£5.95

THE
ALICE BAILEY
INHERITANCE

by

SIR JOHN R. SINCLAIR Bt.

TURNSTONE PRESS LIMITED
Wellingborough, Northamptonshire

First published 1984
Second Impression 1985

British Library Cataloguing in Publication Data

Sinclair, *Sir*, John R.
  The Alice Bailey inheritance.
  1. Life   2. Occult sciences
  I. Title
  133   BF1411

  ISBN 0-85500-177-1

*Turnstone Press is part of the
Thorsons Publishing Group*

Printed and bound in Great Britain

Acknowledgements

A book such as this one is so much of a group effort that the author can justly be regarded as a sort of co-ordinating secretary, and the acknowledgements embrace many whom it is not possible to list here in an individual way. Thanks are due to many, including Alick Bartholomew and Ian Gordon-Brown, who, I, believe, discussed the original idea and looked in my direction; the editorial and other staff at Turnstone-Thorsons Publishing House who have done so much to shape the product; Mary Bailey and the directors of the Lucis Press/Publishing Co. who have generously permitted many quotations from Alice Bailey's original material; my good friends Vera Stanley Alder and Marian Rohe Walter, old co-workers of Alice Bailey, who have provided moral support; Doris Gill and Joyce Green who laboured valiantly checking seemingly endless references, also Christina Forbes and Kate E. Butler for assistance, Frazer Wood whose photographic prowess salvaged old snapshots and Mr M. Scott who typed one version of a draft MSS. Then there are the many publishing houses and other institutions that have kindly given permission for the quotation of complementary and explanatory works of reference. If any remain untraced by the time we go to print, inspite of copious correspondence, such information as we have on them will be found in the bibliographical index, and we acknowledge all these contributory works with gratitude, they include:
The Guildford Muniment Room — Surrey Records Office (photograph of Moor Park).
The Office of His Holiness the Dalai Lama and Phuntsog Wangyal.
H.H. European Representative (*The Principle of Universal Responsibility*).
Princeton University Press (Mircea Eliade, *Shamanism: Archaic*

Techniques of Ecstacy, trans. Willard R. Trask, Bollingen Series LXXXVI, Copyright © 1964).

Dr Ac. Sidney Rose-Neil and the British Acupuncture Assoc. (*Acupuncture and the Life Energies*).

Gaston Saint-Pierre and the Metamorphic Assoc. (*The Metamorphic Technique*, Element Books).

Routledge and Kegan Paul (Gregory Tillett, *The Elder Brother*).

A. M. Heath & Co. Ltd. (Joseph Campbell, *The Masks of God*, Souvenir Press).

Neville Spearman (Harold Saxton Burr, *Blueprints of Immortality*, and John J. O'Neill, *Prodigal Genius: The Life of Nikola Tesla*).

Hutchinson Publishing Group (Gary Zukov, *The Dancing Wu Li Masters*).

Macdonald & Co. (Ursula K. LeGuin, *The Left Hand of Darkness*).

Shambhala Publications, Inc. (The Ven. Chögyam Trungpa Rinpoche, *The Myth of Freedom*).

Faber & Faber, and Harcourt Brace Janovich, Inc. (T. S. Eliot, *Four Quartets — Little Gidding*).

Contents

But who comes now? And what shall be her fate?
For as they leave that state,
Some have I seen in whom love was a flame
So bright that men remembered Whence they came.

—The Angel's speech from *The Cloak* by Clifford Bax

Introduction

Looking back in a few years' time, I believe we may feel indebted to Turnstone for venturing a series of books on some of the seminal influences which underlie the present consciousness-growth movement. The flow of this movement is, after all, a nebulous, though energetic, stirring within society that for want of any more precise banner is sometimes referred to, very loosely, as 'New Age' activity. And although this may be familiar to those who identify themselves with the mainstream of such activity, it is not entirely helpful to the outside investigator who is trying to find out what it all means. Many elements of the present creative germination are deeply rooted in time, and a case can be made for a sequential though chequered progress towards definite goals, dating at least from the days of the European Renaissance and Reformation and, some would say, from an even earlier period than that. [1]

A survey of a few of the channels which have recently released energy to stir us all up and galvanize us creatively can only be useful. So much is in the process of change within the world of the psyche as well as in outer society that a brief referral to source material may have a stabilizing and healing effect. Acquaintances occasionally ask me if the whole (New Age) scene of research, belief systems, alternative therapies, meditation techniques and general exploration into the hidden aspects of 'human beingness' now receiving an increasing public response is as much of a jumble as it sometimes appears to be; or whether there is any coherent design and intelligent pattern trying to surface. The widely varied careers and work-styles of the characters chosen for review in this series must provide, at the very least, a good read. However, it may turn out that to some degree, and albeit through the agency of different terminologies and styles of psychological language, a most interesting flowering of the collective psyche or human soul will be witnessed in action once this set of books is produced in its entirety.

The human race has provided its membership with a mass of fine and intriguing spiritual teachers throughout its history: one does not want to get into the business of special claims. Yet in accepting authorship within this series I feel that I have a responsibility to show why what is sometimes called 'the Bailey work' — a misnomer, as we are talking about one contribution to a broad work-stream that flows to a very wide horizon — should be among the channels chosen for close scrutiny, particularly as Alice Ann Bailey is someone about whom many will have heard nothing whatsoever.

The Ven. Chögyam Trungpa Rinpoche once pointed out in a talk that Christ was not a Christian and Buddha was not a Buddhist; the terms were applied to their followers by others, who doubtless required some sort of ready reference. And I feel sure that few pioneers think of themselves or their work as neatly packaged and labelled. Mrs Bailey chose to prospect life as she found it, in her own way, and had no wish to found any particular cult or system. She simply tried to help others discover a little more of what life was about and also make their own contribution to it increasingly worthwhile.

A great deal of what Alice Bailey involved herself in was deeply subjective, even though the teacher with whom she co-operated once wrote:

You must remember . . . that any person who takes the position that the work to be done is *only* upon the inner planes and that he is working solely from mental or spiritual levels of consciousness is *not* right in his conception of the process. Inner work which does not work out into objective activity upon the physical plane is wrongly oriented and inspired.[2]

In fact, a large part of our story is concerned with the steps Mrs Bailey took to bring her work out into the open in a useful, impersonal, yet caring way. Coupled with this there were in her character traits of extreme shyness and self-effacement. So many purveyors of what has been termed the ageless wisdom[3] are credited with more than a little wildness and flamboyance of personality. As though to redress some hidden balance, A.A.B.

— as we had better refer to her for the sake of brevity — was in many respects the epitome of an English lady (though one must admit that that species can seem as strange to some as the roughest sannyasin does to others). Anyone wanting to obtain more details than this book provides can of course read her own books, including her autobiography, research the body of teaching to which her name has been given or investigate the functional institutions, which I shall mention, that sprang from her ideas.[4] Nevertheless, in the last analysis it will be the fruitage that grows from all these sources that proves their effectiveness. It is perhaps a measure of the growing influence of the items just mentioned that Turnstone should have chosen a relative unknown, about whom so little has been written and about whom so much is yet to be digested, so early on in the series.

I believe, though it is a tough item for any author to discuss, that there should be a word on why I am undertaking this job. It is only fair to the reader that I should state that my qualifications are quite meagre. I am neither an investigative journalist nor a close friend or relative of the Bailey family. And although I did meet Alice Bailey, this happened most briefly, at the end of her life and when I was very young. However, like many others, I did go through the school she founded, and for seven years I worked on the staff administering its affairs. I recall that when I was first invited to do so, an early task I was allotted was that of pruning letters and other documents from the ancient files of former students, some going back years before the world war. I believe I was instructed to keep the most important items, in case any of the individuals concerned chose to rejoin the school at a later date. Although I am sure I sought the advice of anyone with time enough to give a word or two, my decisions on what might be of real significance represented the roughest kind of crash course in developing intuition and learning to make more mistakes than statistics consider proper. Even though I had attempted the work assigned me by the school, I had not then read much of Alice Bailey's material, a detail I could hardly disguise, even though I did not go out of my way to advertise the fact at the time and did hasten to put the matter right.

Nonetheless, a good few hundred files later, little curiosity about other people's shenanigans remained, and I was left with a profound sympathy for anyone trying to follow the so-called 'spiritual path' across those fiery stones provided and set alight by whatever energy they themselves supply out of their own essential nature.

In fact, this is the second occasion on which I have been asked to provide a book discussing A.A.B. and her work. Some years ago, another publisher wanted a biography: it was never written, although I did discuss the possibility with her husband Foster Bailey, who was alive then. This present book is in no way a biography, though it may contain the odd illustrative incident, but what he wrote in the course of our exchange has considerable relevance now:

One of Alice's reasons for writing an autobiography was to prevent a Bailey cult. She pictured herself as no extraordinary person with a mission. Her impelling reason was to encourage other students struggling on the Path by making it clear that they could work as she could work as a disciple. She was a disciple and so also they could be. She faced hardships and so could they. She stuck to it and so could they.

But the autobiography was distasteful to her and she never finished it. At the end she all but abandoned it, leaving it to me to edit and publish as I chose. I chose to leave it unfinished with very little editing and to publish. Alice had hoped that no one would publish her biography after her death. I told her it was probably inevitable, but that we might 'steal the market' by a partial record which showed her as a normal woman who worked hard. She spoke clearly about her work but did not push herself as a leader, and actively discouraged devoteeism, however slight, and never claimed any authority. She was aghast that by error it became known that the Tibetan was a member of the Hierarchy. D.K. reassured her that it would not do the harm she feared. Anyway, the Hierarchy was coming out in due course and exemplified impersonality which to them was useful. I am happy that for 22 years [since her death in 1949 — JRS.] there has been no biography and no Bailey cult.

The message here is as clear as Thomas à Kempis' statement in *The Imitation of Christ* ('The Following of Christ' is the precise translation): 'Ask not who said this, but mark what is said; men pass away, but the truth of the Lord remains forever.' If readers will hold the spirit of this advice in mind, and be prepared to use their own intuition and common sense to cut through the shortcomings of my descriptions, which must as any individual point of view necessarily is be partial, then perhaps through our combined efforts some useful perception may come into focus.

For my part I will discuss as many aspects of this work as may be possible within a compact book; also where possible, I will give a reference for various aspects of the teaching so that those who wish to may check up on some particular within the context. Where it seems useful, I will try to offer illustrative examples from other works which may amplify what is being discussed. Yet, obviously, any individual exploration into a body of work such as that launched via A.A.B. builds upon a series of incidents, conversations and experiences over the years; sometimes I may recall an item and be unable to put a finger on a precise reference, in which case I shall leave readers to digest the material in their own way. They can always, if they wish, apply one of Foster Bailey's favourite phrases: 'Interesting, if true.' This book is not intended as an exercise in propaganda.

Where incidents are mentioned, this is done not to gossip but to show that the ageless wisdom really does have a very human face behind the mask of imagined mystery. And where names are included, this is not done in order to appropriate them to any cause or link them to A.A.B. but to keep our subject flowing freely in a broad context. People often long to box everything they come across into neat mental pigeon-holes; but nature, though basically economical, is not always so tidy. I do hope readers will remember this. (Once when I broke a limb, I complained of the disruption to work: 'Accidents weren't designed to be convenient,' said the nursing sister and left me to proceed as best I could.) Not everything here will fit into your mental horizon at once: give it time to settle.

Because of limitations on space I am going to lead a dive in towards the deep end, so we will begin right away with the difficult questions raised by theosophic labels like 'Hierarchy'. And what on earth does 'coming out' mean in the Foster Bailey context quoted above? What was the function of the Tibetan known as D.K. in relation to the work we are to review? Words such as 'disciple' seem strangely out of keeping with the rough and tumble of our contemporary environment — how shall we interpret them in a practical way? If Alice Bailey was a disciple, of whom and what and why?

John R. Sinclair
London 1982

Alice Ann Bailey.

1. The Inconceivable Mansion of Awakened Perception

With what is rather bald simplicity we will start by listing some of the implications contained in the final sentences of Foster Bailey's statement. And then, within the text of this first chapter we will begin to analyse and consider what they may mean. I say 'begin', because the full extent of these implications is something that the interested reader will need to continue to confront and research long after he or she has laid this book aside.

First, Alice Bailey worked as an amanuensis, a secretary and to some extent a personal assistant to a Tibetan using the *nom de plume* Djwhal Khul. Thirty years of this co-operative activity produced a large amount of teaching of a philosophical, psychological and esoteric nature, published in several lengthy volumes as well as in a number of shorter books. As a result of this teaching a variety of spiritually oriented educational activities came into being. The co-operation was especially remarkable in that both partners carried on their own lives in separate locations and communicated in a largely subjective fashion. Alice Bailey took responsibility for the books but stated that they were by no means 'all her own work'.

Secondly, over the years, because of the quality of the work produced, and for other reasons, an increasing number of people have accepted that Djwhal Khul is associated with the legendary network of *rishis*, saints, guild masters, Enlightened Guardians, *Nautoniers*, Guiding Helmsmen or what have you. According to general beliefs about such adepts, it is understood that, whether in or out of incarnation, they exert their influence on behalf of the spiritual maturing of all sentient beings as well as for the general welfare of the whole planetary life. Therefore, by implication if for no other reason, many people also believe that Alice Bailey motivated her self-disciplined effort to promote a number of useful service activities through her understanding of the caring attitude which pervades this Group, Guild, Lodge, Ashram — whatever one chooses to call this network of goodwill. She herself referred to it collectively as the Hierarchy, in the consideration that its organic structure offers a pathway of ascent or liberation from the frustrating limitations of the human state and an opportunity to realize the full potential of the soul essence or spiritual component within each conscious being.

Thirdly, statements made throughout Alice Bailey's published works indicated that, to some extent at least, this occulted hierarchical group plan in time to walk again the ways of men and offer their combined assistance (formerly the lone pioneer or wise person, operating here or there, appears to have been the usual procedure) in the nurturing and governance of planet earth. This vision was an abiding influence in much that A.A.B. undertook during her life. Having been hidden from the outer scene for an immensely long period of time — so long that often only fragmented rumours of former initiate-kings or of another order of beings remain to hint at their activity — adepts would again emerge into relatively open influence; they would 'come out', as Foster Bailey put it. However, the implications seem to be that such an influence would neither infringe on anyone's spiritual freedom nor supplant the opportunities for self-initiated growth to maturity and realization which life within earth's school affords those willing to make use of its challenging opportunity. No one is encouraged to 'wait for Godot'. 'Mary Poppins' does not clear up the mess in the nursery; we do that for ourselves. The expectation lies in the immense potential that exists for human development as and when we decide to quit fooling around. This, at least, is my own rough and ready comprehension of what Foster had to say to me.

Of course, A.A.B. is by no means the first European teacher to discuss such ideas. If we consider fleetingly only a few instances, we must recall the strange Rosicrucian manifestoes that appeared in the seventeenth century announcing the arrival of 'an invisible brotherhood' in various European cities. This created a furore of excitement, but subsequently the expectations became entangled in the sad events of the Thirty Years War, so that within only a few years they seemed to have been a sort of imaginative romance or shadow play. [1] And yet a seed was sown which drew strength from many Hermetic sources, so that later on these events

The Blavatsky-approved artist's impressions of three teachers interested in the theosophical movement. If one follows through the various hints and statements given in A.A.B's writings, these pictures are of hologram-type projections (mayavirupa); the hologram form being of the physical vehicles, and the period, in which these Lodge members attained adepthood.

seemed almost like a somewhat abortive trial run for theosophical doctrine.

Other intimations of hidden orders, such as Cagliostro's attempt to spread Egyptian rites throughout the masonic movement in Europe, met with even less success. (His work fell victim to the hazards of the French Revolution.[2]) The theosophical teaching of that fiery Russian lady Helena Petrovna Blavatsky, given in the second half of the nineteenth century, built much of its subsequent activity around the idea of hidden Masters of wisdom. Madame Blavatsky allegedly regretted having mentioned their existence,[3] and a large portion of the public, if they picked up the idea at all, either hoped mainly for personal advancement through some new type of guru or found the presentation of the subject somewhat amusing.[4] Yet teachers like Ouspensky continued to hint at the possibility of 'an invisible fraternity', and Madame Helena Roerich, wife of the artist and designer, was quite definite about it.[5]

Amongst all the undoubted nonsense, the thread of a vital concept was maintained by a core of sincere people, and it was this lifeline, against considerable odds as we shall see, that A.A.B. picked up. She had been brought up by various members of her family in strict fundamental Christian households and began her ministry, as soon as she had the choice, as a voluntary evangelical worker in Lily Sandes' soldiers' homes for the British army. She was first stationed in Ireland with Miss Sandes for a period of training, but was soon sent to India as one of the managers for homes there. Years later, when the responsibilities of a family of her own took her out of this work, she was faced with what psychologists sometimes call a 'mid-life crisis' that hit at all levels, as these experiences tend to, on the break-up of her first marriage. She was left, without physical or emotional support, to look after her three young children in America, well away from her influential family. And it was at this testing moment, while working her way through her very tangible problem and holding down a tough employment, that she came under the tutelage of two of Madame Blavatsky's own personal students. From there she found her way, for a relatively short period, into the mainstream of Theosophical Society activity at their centre at Krotona in Hollywood.[6]

However, years before any of this took place and before she was acquainted with any theosophical concepts, a somewhat exceptional experience had set its mark on the work into which she now advanced. On Sunday 30 June 1895, [7] while staying at the home of an aunt in Kirkcudbrightshire, Scotland, she received a surprise visit from someone whom nearly twenty-five years on she identified as a messenger from that aspect of the company of adepts sometimes called the Blue Lodge or, more specifically, that section of it known as the trans-Himalayan branch of a creative Hierarchy. [8] She recorded her considerable astonishment and alarm when this individual walked into the room where she was sitting. Fifteen years old at the time, she had for some reason remained in the house when the rest of the party went out to attend the morning Church service. She recalled the messenger's personal admonishments — for she was rather severe with herself and admitted to having had a difficult adolescence — and that he mentioned some future work. His look, the turban he wore and the fact that his European clothes were very well cut were all remembered. The meeting was short, and few other details, according to her own account, remained with her. [9] She kept the experience to herself as she had attended revivalist meetings and did not wish to be accused of any form of religious hysteria, having witnessed what could happen.

At the Theosophical Society headquarters she recognized a picture of the messenger and was imprudent enough to mention this interview. As it was then customary for a senior official of the Society to advise members on their spiritual contacts, the revelation did not go down at all well. [10] Not long after this, in November 1919, Djwhal Khul invited her to co-operate in some work with him; and although she at first refused, she later agreed to experiment and finally, after some discussion, accepted. [11] This led to the production of her writings and to much that emerged as a result of them over a period of thirty years. In effect, she worked as an amanuensis, which according to the Penguin Dictionary is simply 'a secretary, copyist or literary assistant'. The unusual aspect of the work, as we have noted, was that her principal was in another place and their often daily communications took place telepathically. It was on this count that A.A.B.'s initial objections arose: by her own admission she was prejudiced against anything that smacked of psychic phenomena, and this activity, although it must have grown out of her own meditative work and the techniques she had been taught, appeared too like automatic writing to appeal to her.

The first two books, *Initiation, Human and Solar* and *Letters on Occult Meditation* contained in simple form much that was later expanded into a far more subtle and sophisticated form. One can speculate that had the experiment aborted at that point, at least a seed of the whole exposition would have been grounded. The early chapters of *Initiation, Human and Solar* were sent to the world headquarters of the Theosophical Society at Adyar, India, for P.B. Wadia to publish in *The Theosophist*. It is quite possible that it was here that the substance of a comment by Gregory Tillett, C.W. Leadbeater's biographer, had its root:

One possible origin for some of the material in [Leadbeater's] *The Masters and the Path*, and for material on the Occult Hierarchy and Initiations lies in a wholly unexpected source. Although she was regarded as 'misguided' because she had both left the TS and claimed to be inspired by a Master, Alice Bailey held a fascination for some Theosophists from the time she began her independent career outside the Society in 1920-1. Leadbeater owned, read and regarded highly her earlier works, and although she was criticized officially within the Society for 'falsely' claiming to be in communication with D.K. and others, Leadbeater did not criticize her. The material in her first 'inspired' book, *Initiation, Human and Solar*, bears an interesting similarity to some of Leadbeater's work, in content though not in style. One wonders which came first. [12]

In fact, the question is apparently foreseen and replied to in the fifth volume of Alice Bailey's *A Treatise on the Seven Rays, The Rays and The Initiations*, where it is written:

If these new phases of the teaching have been later given to the public by other occult groups, it will have been because the information was gained by those who have read the books put out by A.A.B. for me or who are directly and consciously in touch with my Ashram.

An instance of this is that book by C.W. Leadbeater on *The Masters and the Path* which was published later than my book, *Initiation, Human and Solar*. If the dates of any given teaching are compared with that given by me, it will appear to be of a later date than mine. I say this with no possible interest in any controversy among occult groups or the interested public, but as a simple statement of fact and as a protection to this particular work of the Hierarchy. [13]

A number of different techniques were reportedly employed in the production of A.A.B.'s many books. [14] The first two books, already mentioned, were dictated; this also happened with certain difficult esoteric passages, such as 'The Stanzas of Dzyan' to be found in *A Treatise on Cosmic Fire*, which were given 'audibly' word for word. Sometimes on such occasions, Foster Bailey related, another presence could be sensed, though not physically seen. He also remarked that the Tibetan, as D.K. was usually referred to, had some initial difficulty with fluency in the English language and it was therefore of value to have the co-operation of the Western-educated mind of A.A.B. I recall that Foster collected an unwitting laugh on one occasion when he said: 'After working with Alice for some time, the Tibetan's language improved.'

Certain symbols were visualized through a form of clairvoyance, and other material such as mantras and charts came through in memory out of the sleep state, when consciousness can be active outside the physical form. (I understand from Dr Shafica Karagulla MD that she has in preparation a book entitled *Through the Curtain*, which records and evaluates this kind of experience.) However, as the work progressed, the vast bulk of material was transmitted by a harmonious connection between the two co-operating minds which allowed A.A.B.'s physical brain to produce the written material at high speed. The image one gets is not unlike that of a rather sensitive modern computer transcribing a document programme fed through it. When she was working in this way, she had a little stock of sharpened pencils at the ready.

Later, when the teaching had gathered its own adherents, this method of writing led to a certain amount of conjecture. Readers might have been attracted to a particular item of information, and yet found another statement unacceptable. On such occasions, rather than have their own comfort in what they wished to believe removed, they insisted that A.A.B. had twisted the meaning and got it down wrongly. For her, naturally enough, it was a point of honour to put everything down exactly as she had received it. And, as she pointed out, huge areas of the subject matter were quite obviously outside her field of knowledge.[15] This problem is quite a frequent one, and appears in various shapes and sizes whenever people are confronted by that peculiar psychological struggle whereby they wish to avoid denting their faith in a particular source but find certain items mentally indigestible. At the time Mary Lutyens took over responsibility for editing J. Krishnamurti's writings and for preparing them for book form, I believe a similar problem arose when his *Freedom from the Known* appeared. An accomplished authoress herself, she was suspected of making alterations; in fact, what devotees had come up against was her professionalism as an editor.

Of course, where translation from one language to another is concerned, there may indeed be very real problems because of a lack of precisely similar words in either tongue. A Dutch linguist, Gerhard Jansen, who supervised the translation of many A.A.B. scripts had an especial headache, particularly when translators fell out with one another over interpretation. This is a well-known problem in all sorts of technical fields, without the added concern of esoteric concepts. When international conferences so often rely on instantaneous translation, many specialized agencies using specific terminology, or even language that can have several meanings, find it cheaper to fly in experienced translators than risk misinterpretation. For instance, the word 'border' or 'frontier' could be translated into a given language in such a way as to have a more military connotation than the speaker intended, with the consequence that suspicions may arise. This being so, it is not difficult to imagine the problems that can arise when non-professionals, however brilliant, tackle highly abstruse scripts, not on a fee-paid basis but out of the goodness of their hearts. One of Foster Bailey's many stories related to the first edition of *A Treatise on White Magic* when the printers inadvertently typeset twenty pages of the material twice over. So new and difficult to digest were many of the ideas contained in those pages that it was two years before anyone, including the Baileys, discovered the error — and this occurred in the original English version.

A.A.B. wrote a preface to the third book, which was also the first treatise (this one was on cosmic fire, while others were concerned with the seven rays and the aforesaid white magic) she produced, in which she asked students to approach the text with sympathetic sincerity of thought, common-sense discrimination and spiritual intuition. She concluded her remarks with a passage from *The Secret Doctrine* (this treatise having been dedicated to Madame Blavatsky), which concerned ideas attributed to the Buddha:

The Lord Buddha has said that we must not believe in a thing said merely because it is said; nor traditions because they have been handed down from antiquity; nor rumours, as such; nor writings by sages, because sages wrote them; nor fancies that we may suspect to have been inspired in us by a Deva (that is, in presumed spiritual inspiration); nor from inference drawn from some haphazard assumption we may have made; nor because of what seems an analogical necessity; nor on the mere authority of our teachers or masters. But we are to believe when the writing, doctrine, or saying is corroborated by our own reason and consciousness. 'For this,' says he in concluding, 'I taught you not to believe merely because you have heard, but when you believed of your consciousness, then to act accordingly and abundantly. [16]

A number of quite popular books are circulating at the present time, for which the authors named on the jackets have acted as an amanuensis of some sort. The 'Gildas' and the 'Seth' books often adopt the practice of giving an account of the 'sittings' at which scripts were produced. This has been practical because these books were, in both cases, the work of a team. In one case, Ruth White had the support of Mary Swainson as note-taker; and in the other, Jane Roberts' husband plays secretary while his wife speaks for Seth, this type of dictation being quite distinct from the books Mrs Roberts wrote under her own name. [17] In the case of Ruth White, she is able to describe Gildas and sometimes sees him at work in his more subtle energy nature when providing a connection between healing groups; one here on the physical plane supported by another from a different level, it would seem. And on one occasion, in answer to a question of Mary Swainson's, in what they called 'after dinner conversation' (as opposed to a strict focus on special subject matter) they measured the image seen of Gildas by making a pencil mark on the wall. [18]

The material in *A Course in Miracles*, though anonymous, was reportedly written over several years by a trained psychological worker in a manner closely resembling automatic writing: that is, like Geraldine Cummins's books, they could be written while the scribe's conscious mind was apparently participating in some other activity. In Miss Cummins's case, she was able to hold a conversation while busily writing on a completely different subject. And in the case of *A Course in Miracles*, when a gap in transmission was necessary the written flow would pick up precisely at the point where it had been stopped earlier. As the entire script was produced to its own particular rhythm so that each sentence apparently arrived as a completed part of the whole text, the reader is confronted by a production that is remarkable by any standards, regardless of whether the subject matter appeals or not.

This work started after a series of what, in the jargon of some modern psychological techniques, are called 'guided daydreams', some of which, I believe, continued even while the participant was on public transport, thereby illustrating the capacity of consciousness to be active at more than one level at once. This sequence of inner visioning was followed by a disturbing urge to write — disturbing, because the scribe in question, like A.A.B., felt a strong hesitation. [19] In this case also there appears the familiar figure of the companion-in-work or partner, a professional colleague who vetted the scripts, originally, for any sign of mental imbalance. After some six years, two large books, one of text and the other containing daily lessons with meditative exercises for a year (or longer, as the student is left to decide his or her own pace), plus a slimmer volume for teachers, had been produced. These were handed over, after discussion, to Judith Skutch (of the Foundation for Inner Peace) and Douglas Dean, who then found themselves with the responsibility of publishing and circulating the material and generally playing 'Aaron' so that the anonymity of the original 'Moses' could be preserved.

Enough strange stories exist in the world to indicate that the potential ramifications and abilities of consciousness are a good deal wider than our customary personified packaging allows. There are clearly (or perhaps not so clearly, in the opinion of some people) psychological mysteries relating to human identity, which are as tantalizing as any lost continent. Once again, the language of computer technology offers a model from which some understanding can come, if we are prepared to consider this type of amenuensis as an unique item of hierarchical 'hardware' (a description A.A.B. might readily have accepted, by all accounts).

The co-operation between the Tibetan and A.A.B. was at the same time more ordinary and yet more rare than the recent cases of inspired writing which we have described above, albeit rather superficially. In that both participants were stated to be alive in physical bodies at the time of their work together, the idea of their combined efforts is no more unusual than Robert Angus Downie's considerable work for Sir James Frazer (of *Golden Bough* renown) after that famous author went blind. That they were several thousand miles apart, and that the flow of telepathic dictation relied on them making contact at times when their everyday activities allowed them both to give the required focus in order to get onto the necessary vibratory wavelength — if I may put it in these rather inexact words — and this over a period of thirty years of steady work, looks very like a unique record.

Besides the various books that were written there was also a series of letters of instruction given to personal students of Djwhal Khul. We look at this aspect of the work briefly in another chapter; for the moment, however, it may be useful to consider how D.K. viewed the operation from his side:

I wonder if any of you really grasp the extent of the effort which I have to make in order to reach your minds and teach you? When, for instance, I seek to send out these instructions I have to make the following preparation. First, I seek to ascertain the mental state and preparedness of the amanuensis, A.A.B., and whether the press of the other work upon which she is engaged in connection with the Plan of the spiritual Hierarchy permits of her right reception; for if the work is exerting extreme pressure and if she is occupied with urgent problems, it may be needful for me to wait until such time as circumstances give her the needed leeway both of time and strength, and of mental detachment. My own sphere of occult work must also come under consideration. Then, having established a rapport with her, I have three things to do.

First, I must gather the group of disciples as a whole into my aura and so gauge its general condition of receptivity — for that must determine the scope of the intended communication. Do you realize, my brothers, that as you extend your power to grasp the needed lessons and learn to train your minds to think in ever wider and more abstract terms, you draw from me a correspondingly adequate instruction? The limitation to the imparted truth lies on your side and not on mine.

Second, I must isolate in my own consciousness the extent of the instruction, detaching myself from all other concerns and formulating the needed material into a thought-form which will be comprehensive, clear-cut, sequential in its relation to that which has already been imparted and which will lay the ground for the next instruction in due time.

Then third, I have to enter into that meditative condition, and that extraverted attitude which will enable me to pour out in a steady stream of constructive sentences which will express, to the mind of the amanuensis, the thoughtform as I see it and build it. Putting it otherwise, I become creative with deliberation and endeavour to convey to the vision, to the mind and to the intellectual perception of A.A.B. an ordered presentation of the thought-form which embodies the lesson I desire the students to learn.

All this necessitates an expenditure of force and of time on my part which I feel is well warranted if the students — on their side — will prepare their minds, give the needed time, respond to the few requests I may make, and eventually co-operate with the work of bringing the edited instructions to the attention of aspirants and disciples everywhere and later to a wider public. [20]

When the phenomena was discussed with him (though not, unfortunately, by A.A.B. herself), the psychologist Carl Jung allegedly considered that the Tibetan could be an aspect of Alice Bailey's own consciousness, possibly — and this is my supposition of his opinion, not his — in much the same way that that great man seems to have considered his dialogues with Philomen took place as part and parcel of his own awareness [21]; or again, possibly in the sense in which he recognized two, inner and outer, levels of his personality as a young man. [22]

A.A.B.'s response to this was that she could not have received a physical parcel from an aspect of her own consciousness, and by means of a third party. As this is a rather peculiar story, it is perhaps best given in her own account:

A few years ago a very dear friend and a man who stood very closely with Foster and me since the inception of our work — Mr Henry Carpenter — went out to India to try and reach the Masters at Shigatze, a small, native town in the Himalayas, just over the Tibetan frontier. He made this effort three times in spite of my telling him that he could find the Masters right here in New York if he took the proper steps and the time was ripe. He felt he would like to tell the Masters, much to my amusement, that I was having too tough a time and that They had better do something about it. As he was a personal friend of Lord Reading, once Viceroy of India, he was given every facility to reach his destination but the Dalai Lama refused permission for him to cross the frontier. During his second trip to India when at Gyan(g)tse (the farthest point he could reach near the frontier) he heard a great hubbub in the compound of the dak bungalow. He went to find out what it was and found a lama, seated on a donkey, just entering the compound. He was attended by four lamas and all the natives in the compound were surrounding them and bowing. Through his interpreter, Mr Carpenter made inquiries and was told that the lama was the abbot of a monastery across the Tibetan frontier and that he had come down especially to speak to Mr Carpenter.

The abbot told him that he was interested in the work that we were doing and asked after me. He inquired about the Arcane School and gave him two large bundles of incense for me. Later, Mr Carpenter saw General Laden Lha at Darjeeling. The General is a Tibetan, educated in Great Britain at public school and university and was in charge of the secret service on the Tibetan frontier. He is now dead but was a great and good man. Mr Carpenter told him of his experience with this lama and told him that he was the abbot of a certain lamaserie. The General flatly denied the possibility of this. He said the abbot was a very great and holy man and that he had never been known to come down across the frontier or visit an Occidental. When, however, Mr Carpenter returned the following year, General Laden Lha admitted that he had made a mistake; and that the abbot had been down to see him. [23]

The incense existed for all to see, and smell, as the fragrance was pleasantly strong. I thought it would be a good idea to have it analysed; however, quite aside from the difficulty of finding a chemist to undertake the task, Tibetan incense from the Nepalese region can sometimes be made up of a combination of as many as thirty-six herbs, so I do not think the result would have been particularly satisfactory. In any event, the point of this account emphasizes D.K.'s physical presence.

It is also evident from this story that A.A.B. knew the Tibetan teacher whom she worked with under more than one name, as presumably did others. As we have stated, his 'professional' name as author, and one that was popular in theosophical circles, was Djwhal Khul. The name he used in his official function within the structure of his religious duties was kept confidential. There are probably other names as well; there is nothing particularly new or extraordinary about the business of having different names for different states or functions. The Egyptian pharaohs reportedly had a number of names: a secret spiritual name, their royal title, a dynastic name, their own family name, the name they might be called by intimates, and perhaps, as many people do, a pet name as well. [24] That, of course, is only an example taken rather at random; we could all think of others. What we have rather lost at the present time is the ability to use names with power, though there are those who manage to empower their names in the sense of 'having a name' within certain circles, and this can help with influencing events, assist in business negotiations or even affect the amount of money an individual is paid. I am acquainted with one internationally known writer who insists on formal address, unless specific permission has been given to someone to use the first name, because of a belief that it carries a very personal and private vibration.

Yet once again we must remind ourselves of the advice of St Thomas à Kempis quoted in the introduction. The whole tenor of A.A.B.'s teaching material, even where it was directed towards particular individuals in whom D.K. was interested, is distinguished by an impersonality which is difficult for the human personality, with its daily efforts at gaining recognition, to comprehend. The state of adepthood is veiled in seemingly egoless identity, a quality of life which is somewhat outside our customary experience. The emergence of the Hierarchy can, I think, be accepted as rather more than its 'coming out' of some secret closet. D.K. tried to discuss some of the practicalities of this potential spiritual emergence which he referred to as 'the externalization'.

Though the Masters of the Wisdom have all passed through the human experience and are simply men who have achieved a relative measure of perfection, there are aspects of physical contact which They have completely transcended and utterly negated. There is nothing in the three worlds with which They have any affinity, except the affinity of life and the impulse of love for all beings. Recovery of certain facilities of activity has been deemed necessary. For instance, the five senses, where a Master is concerned, exist and are used at need, but the contact established and maintained with disciples and senior aspirants in the world (through whom They primarily work) is largely telepathic; hearing and sight, as you understand their uses, are not involved. The science of impression, with its greatly increased effectiveness over individual contact through the senses, has entirely superseded the more strictly human method. Except in the case of Masters working on the physical plane and in a physical body, the outer physical senses are in abeyance; for the majority of Masters who still use these senses, the use is strictly limited; Their work is still almost entirely subjective and the mode of telepathic interplay and of impression is practically all the means which They employ to reach Their working agents. [25]

Apropos of the above, one friend had an intriguing experience when asking, in silent prayer, for some assistance on the way. Into mind came a clear directive to look up Act III, sc.iii of Shakespeare's *King John*, where the following text was found:

> Hear me without thine ears, and make reply
> Without a tongue, using conceit (concept) alone,
> Without eyes, ears, and harmful sound of words;
> Then, in despite of brooded watchful day,
> I would into thy bosom pour my thoughts.

Elsewhere, D.K. stated: 'It is, for instance, less of an effort for me to contact you than it would be for some of the Chohans . . . I am nearer to you, because I am still utilizing the same physical body in which I took the fifth initiation, nearly ninety years ago (recorded in 1945). [26] Chohans have taken a still higher initiation and are focal points of powerful ashrams; Their task of adjustment is very much harder.' This sort of remark has more than a touch of the Shangri-la story [27] about it, and although he also wrote [28] of the crystallization of mind, emotion and physical body that can speed ageing, no clear secret on the subject of longevity is given away. Tibetan Buddhism however is not without beliefs that certain qualities of meditation can help the individual to absorb those universal energies that sustain life and vitality. [29] The subject of expansion of consciousness or initiation into new life experience and understanding is one which D.K. wrote about continuously. A.A.B.'s books are peppered with references to it, and the fifth and final volume of *A Treatise on the Seven Rays* is subtitled *The Rays and the Initiations.*

Is there such a thing as genuinely 'universal' consciousness and realized understanding of life, people may well ask? Even if the answer seems to be that the possibility is a matter of degree, any practitioners of resulting attitudes would be among the most decentralized beings on the planet. Evans-Wentz, the renowned writer on Tibetan secret doctrine, encapsulated this stance in a phrase which has lodged in my memory — and I regret that I quote it from there, without exact reference: 'The Enlightened Ones, by emitting upon the world of phenomena, the radiance of their all embracing love, cause the growth and maturity of all beings that live.' At an Arcane School conference dinner after her death, Foster Bailey made plain the extent to which such a Lodge of enlightened persons motivated the entire *raison d'etre* for A.A.B.'s life's work. [30]

Suggestions for contacting the enlightened ones have been in circulation for centuries and in one form are freely available to the general public in Patanjali's instructions for raja yoga. This particular 'means of union' is sometimes referred to as 'the kingly science of the mind', though A.A.B. prefers the phrase 'the kingly science of the soul'.[31] As this is relevant to our subject, here are two different translations of Sutra 32 from Patanjali's *Book III*, with two different commentaries for comparison. The first is by Charles Johnston; the second by Alice Bailey herself. The passages in this section of Patanjali's work discuss the technicality of what he calls 'the light in the head'. Other practitioners of meditation may use slightly different terms, but as Patanjali has produced four books to explain his way of looking at things, we will not go into that here.

Through perfectly concentrated meditation on the light in the head comes the vision of the Masters who have attained.

The tradition is that there is a certain centre of force in the head, perhaps the 'pineal gland', which some of our western philosophers have supposed to be the dwelling of the soul, a centre which is, as it were, the doorway between the natural and the spiritual man. It is the seat of that better and wiser consciousness behind the outward looking consciousness in the forward part of the head; that better and wiser consciousness of 'the back of the mind', which views spiritual things and seeks to impress the spiritual view on the outward looking consciousness in the forward part of the head. It is the spiritual man seeking to guide the natural man, seeking to bring the natural man to concern himself with the things of his immortality. This is suggested in the words of the Upanishad already quoted. 'There where the dividing of the hair turns, extending upward to the crown of the head'; all of which may sound very fantastical, until one comes to understand it.

It is said that when this power is fully awakened, it brings a vision of the great Companions of the spiritual man, those who have already attained, crossing over to the further shore of the sea of death and rebirth. Perhaps it is to this divine sight that the Master alluded, who is reported to have said: 'I counsel you to buy of me eye salve, that you may see'.[32]

Those who have attained self-mastery can be seen and contacted through focusing the light in the head. This power is developed in one-pointed meditation.

This is a paraphrase of a very general nature, but gives the exact sense of the terms employed. In the twenty-fifth sutra we considered the nature of the light in the head. Here it might briefly be stated that when the aspirant is aware of the light in the head, and can utilize it at will, turning its radiance upon all that he seeks to know, the time comes when he can not only turn it *outward* on to the field of knowledge wherein he functions in the three worlds, but can turn it inward and direct it upward into those realms wherein the saints of God, the great 'Cloud of Witnesses' walk. He can, therefore, through its medium, become aware of the world of the Masters, Adepts and Initiates and thus contact them in full waking consciousness, registering those contacts with his physical brain apparatus.

Hence the necessity of becoming aware of one's own light, of trimming one's lamp, and of using the light that is in one, to the full. By use and care, the power of the spiritual light grows and waxes and develops a dual function.

The aspirant becomes a light or lamp set in a dark place and illumines the way for others. Only thus can the light within be fanned to a flame. This process of lighting others and being a lamp must always precede that wonderful experience wherein the mystic turns his lamp and light into other realms and finds the 'way of escape' into those worlds where the Masters work and walk.

This point needs emphasis for there is too strong an inclination among students to search for the Masters or some Guru or Teacher who will 'give' them light. They can only be found by the one who has lit his own light, trimmed his own lamp and thus provided himself with the means of penetrating into Their world. The more technical side of this matter has been well covered in the words of W. Q. Judge: 'There are two inferences here which have nothing to correspond to them in modern thought. One is, that there is a light in the head; and the other, that there are divine beings who may be seen by those who thus concentrate upon the "light in the head". It is held that a certain nerve, or psychic current, called Brahmarandhra-nadi, passes out through the brain near the top of the head. In this there collects more of the luminous principle in nature than elsewhere in the body and it is called jyotis — the light in the head. And, as every result is to be brought about by the use of appropriate means, the seeing of divine beings can be accomplished by concentration upon that part of the body more nearly connected with them. This point — the end of Brahmarandhra-nadi — is also the place where the connection is made between man and the solar forces.'

It is this light which causes the 'face to shine' and is responsible for the halo depicted around the head of all saints and Masters and which is seen by those with clairvoyant vision around the head of all advanced aspirants and disciples.

Dviviedi also gives the same teaching in the following words:

'The light in the head is explained to be that collective flow of the light of sattva which is seen at the Brahmarandhra which is variously supposed to be somewhere near the coronal artery, the pineal gland, or over the medulla oblongata. Just as the light of a lamp burning within the four walls of a house presents a luminous appearance at the keyhole, so even does the light of sattva show itself at the crown of the head. This light is very familiar to all acquainted even slightly with Yoga practices and is seen even by concentration on the space between the eyebrows. By Samyama (meditation) on this light the class of beings called siddhas — popularly known in theosophic circles as Mahatmas or high adepts — able to walk through space unseen, are immediately brought to view, notwithstanding obstacles of time and space.'[33]

The spontaneous visioning of siddhas discussed in these quotations has its reflective counterpart in those meditative exercises whereby a particular buddha, saint or teacher may be visualized in the course of religious practice. Particularly in Eastern religious art, there are pictures of meditation masters with a little cloud or nimbus above the head showing that which is sometimes taken to be a higher aspect of themselves and is sometimes identified as a particular spiritual being within whose lineage they may work and function.

Elsewhere,[34] D.K. reiterates the concern of the Lodge, in all relationships with disciples and aspirants as well as with the interested public, for:
1. teaching them to know themselves;
2. setting them free from authority by awakening interest and enquiry in their minds, and then indicating — not more than that — the direction in which the answer should be sought;
3. giving them those conditions which will force them to stand on their own feet and rely on their own souls, and not on any human being, be he a beloved friend, teacher or a Master of the Wisdom.

As stated, the second Patanjali commentary quoted above was written by A.A.B. herself, after the Tibetan had given her his own translation of the yoga-sutras. She was at pains to prove that someone who did so-called psychic work had an intelligence of her own; and three of her published titles, *From Intellect to Intuition*, *The Soul and its Mechanism* and *From Bethlehem to Calvary* (a title inspired by a La Gallienne poem) are, as the saying goes, all her own work. I expect we all know people who balance their workaday job with some out-of-hours creative effort that evokes their interest and expands their talents and, incidentally, demonstrates to themselves and to anyone interested that they are more than they might at first appear to be. Mary Cadogen, for example, who has been secretary of the Krishnamurti Foundation for many years, has produced several books as an independent author. Moreover, in what has been described as an increasingly 'activity-based' modern society, paid employment — for those who have it — can be merely an access to cash flow, while other activities receive more of the heart's attention. Those who can integrate inner and outer work-streams often consider themselves fortunate.

This stated capacity of the light in the head to act as a revealer should not imply that the Masters are in some celestial zoo, waiting to be visited on Sunday afternoons; they are not pictured like the Maeterlinck grandparents in *The Blue Bird* who 'woke up' when somebody thought of them, living only in the re-collection of others. Throughout D.K.'s material, whether in the simpler early writings or the more sophisticated works published later, he indicated that members of the Lodge have their own lives and activities quite independent of what may be known and written about them. Nor are they really hidden, except by our perception; they are not, in the accepted sense, a secret fraternity.

Some years ago the British humorous magazine *Punch* printed a series called 'Popular Misconceptions' drawn, I think, by the cartoonist Pont. I recall a delightful picture of a small girl who was firmly wedged between two aunts in a church pew. The caption read, 'The people in the row behind', and this was filled with the most marvellously fantastical monsters that good manners, and aunts, forbade her to turn round and examine and whom she had presumably judged by their hymn singing. So it is that something outside our immediate perception gathers peculiar and glamorous properties for good or ill. Nowadays, when reincarnated Tibetan Rinpoches can be found visiting most of our major cities, when religious and philosophical leaders travel the world, and when teachers and gurus of all grades and descriptions are visibly hard at work contributing what energy is in them to reform society, the idea of spiritual Masters is hardly mysterious. With an almost gluttonous capacity, we simply absorb the fact of their efforts into the commonplace.

If one can consider anything as paradoxical as objective abstract thinking, then we are trying here to deal with much more than personal spiritual guides or with directors of specific organizations engaged in visionary work, important and valuable though these things may be. I wrote just now of egolessly decentralized consciousness: this is something that is far from easy to come to grips with, and yet it pervades our study of A.A.B's experience. We are, in a sense, trying to conceive of identities who could act like acupressure points on the great life-streams, meridians or lineages which inspire and enliven human culture. In his *Acupuncture and the Life Energies*, Sidney Rose-Neil writes: 'Acupuncture works by stimulating, organising, sedating, rebalancing the body's electro-magnetic forces.' And further: 'We cannot consider that there is only one form of such force in nature, or in the human organism. There may well be hundreds, if not thousands, of different forms of energy, which the organism utilises.'[35].

Those who try to heal and help the organism that is our planetary society, could be visualized as working in a similar way. And these shepherds of the life force are, A.A.B. maintained, great companions, not 'Big Brothers' in the Orwellian sense.

When Alice Bailey was the unknown Mrs Evans and that first marriage went on the rocks, she became for a time what social workers would now call 'a battered wife'.[36] And when, during her third pregnancy, she was knocked downstairs, no big Godfather appeared with shining sword; she worked her own way through her own problem. Such protection as she had came — as it could have done for anyone in a similar predicament if they were fortunate — from alert and caring neighbours in the community in which she found herself.

I sometimes wonder if, in the period before Mr Gurdjieff's book *Meetings with Remarkable Men* (recently made into a film) was published, there were not quite a few people who hoped for an account of fabulous teachers to whom they could go for solace and advice. Certainly, Gurdjieff wrote about teachers; but often enough these were individuals of all kinds whom he met in the rough and tumble of life and with whom he established an essence connection so that the heart of being was sparked and stirred. True, D.K. worked with A.A.B. to make available certain specific volumes of teaching, but he was not her personal teacher or guru. She remained connected with the household of the one who contacted her in 1895. There is an expression in Indian yogic practice which I am not sure quite how to spell but which, being translated, means 'keeping good company', and naturally enough, good companions can teach us much. However, A.A.B. does not appear as being in an 'in-class' experience with the Tibetan;

during the two years of her early life that she spent working on behalf of Miss Sandes in Baluchistan he made no attempt to contact her; they co-operated, when the time was ripe, for specific work. Teaching came, as it does for everyone, from life.[37] The family cook who sat on her bed after work was done and endeavoured to pierce the overlay of fundamentalist Church doctrine with which her childhood environment conditioned the outer or concrete aspect of the mind, was a teacher.[38] When she gently shook the young Alice by the shoulders and said: 'Will you ever learn, Miss Alice, that there are twelve gates into the Holy City and everybody in the world will come in by one or other of them? They will all meet in the market-place but not everyone is going in by your gate,' she gave a lesson A.A.B. did not forget and repeated often from the lecture platform.

The factor of outer and inner aspects of the mind (or higher and lower, if that conceptual image pleases you better) is quite interesting and also quite important. We will discuss the possibility of the two aspects working in tandem, like two ventricles, in another chapter. For the moment it is worth noting that A.A.B. allegedly came into incarnation with a specific job to do and a project to launch.[39] Yet, while her early life indicates a marked tendency to serve and teach, her personality was thoroughly conditioned by the environment into which she had been born. By her own admission, her outlook was extremely narrow, and while eminently sincere, her interpretation of Christianity was based on the strictest Church doctrine.[40] She gradually had to free herself from this thraldom before she could proceed with her inwardly chosen work. Part of the task for all of us, when we hope for increased creativity, is to recognize how conditioned our mental substance is from the moment of our birth. Simply becoming aware of this fact and witnessing the multitude of ways and influences by which it happens seems essential to our recognition of what could be called the 'Is-ness' of things and to our becoming objective in outlook. I mentioned, in passing, Krishnamurti's work *Freedom from the Known*, and although there are those who say they find his approach hard to comprehend, his contribution in releasing creative energy from thraldom is, in my opinion, quite remarkable.

We will meet this subject of inner freedom again; it inevitably becomes an issue in any research into the existence of those who are already free. Having mentioned it now, we will deal first with the subject of phantoms and shadow play. Fantasy can operate at a number of different levels. It can be used consciously as a stepping stone to works of creative imagination. However, if we are not prepared to confront the whole subject of conditioning and make some attempt to understand the ramifications of our own psyche and the many games our thoughts and feelings can play with us, how are we going to arrive at any balanced perception of what is happening around us? There is a be-glamouring 'astral light' within us, as well as the capacity for enlightened perception; motive seems to be a key to right usage.

A great many of the reflective exercises offered in A.A.B.'s teaching work involve visualization. To undertake this in freedom and with understanding means that one has to go quite deeply into the whole business of the creation of thought-forms, those mental patterns, matrixes or formulas which influence our actions constructively and destructively as the case may be. A.A.B.'s book, *A Treatise on White Magic* deals with this subject extensively. Throughout D.K. never avoided pointing out that one can build false images and idols in all sorts of substances and throughout the entire mental, emotional and physical spectrum. D.K. also stated clearly that on occasion there were false images created of himself and of many other Masters. [41] One great acid test is impersonality; is the effect of the vision sensed one of liberating, impersonal inspiration, or is the appeal a subtle attempt to stimulate and ensnare the ego? When giving advice on psychic training, and in a latter to one of his students, D.K. pointed out that a great deal of misapplied though, I suppose, understandable devotion to himself had created a thought-form of him which could be contacted psychially and appeared to be an independent entity. [42] In fact, he stated, this phantom shell was in no way used by himself and merely served to reflect the innocuous and self-flattering platitudes projected by others.

For an entirely separate and different account of how such things can come about, readers should look at Alexandra David-Neal's classic book *With Magic and Magicians in Tibet*. D.K. also advised, in a similar context, that he was not on the outlook for new stenographers because there was 'masses of undigested material with which to work'. [43] And while such a remark need not inhibit anyone from teaching if they have it in them to produce anything helpful, it seems to me that this implies a simple and no doubt heartfelt request that individuals should not lay their trip on him or ask him to take the rap for what is rightly their responsibility.

A modern instance of a phantom phenomenon has been recorded in *The Story of Ruth* by Dr Morton Schatzman (also made into a television play), in which the subject was reportedly able to create apparitions of people so lifelike to her brain that they could allegedly be touched and smelt, could block out light and cast shadow. [44] The theosophist A. P. Sinnett, wrote of the *maya-rupa* or 'shell doomed to die'. [45] The term *maya-rupa* can also be a temporary body of illusion or 'not that' (D.K. also dealt with handling maya [46]) of use in the way one might employ a mask in a play or pageant, which could be illuminating or deceptive as the case might be, or alternatively as a transient artefact created for purposes of communication — a concept not so impossible to entertain now that we are accustomed to the idea of holograms projected on beams of light.

D.K.'s comments on the subject, stretch intuitive understanding as usual, especially where he discusses the master who has been resurrected on the mountain-top and has 'ascended' to the buddhic level, 'from which plane he must permanently work and not just occasionally, as has been the method hitherto.'

He can work through a physical body (with its subtler sheaths) or not, as he sees fit. He realises that he, as an individual, no longer needs a physical body or an astral consciousness, and that the mind is only a *service instrument*. The body in which he now functions is a body of light which has its own type of substance. The Master, however, can build a body through which He can approach His incoming disciples and those who have not taken the higher initiations; He will normally build this body in semblance of the human form, doing so instantaneously and by an act of the will, when required. The majority of the Masters who are definitely working with humanity either preserve the old body in which They took the fifth initiation or else They build the 'mayavirupa' or body of maya, of physical substance. This body will appear in the original form in which They took initiation. [45]

A member of the Lodge who is often referred to by the letter R., for Rakoczi [47] and who is described in general theosophical literature, as well as in A.A.B.'s writings, as a European Master whose public work in reported former incarnations has been relatively recent, appears to have been quite ill-served in this respect, even allowing for the fact that reports of his public appearances in Europe take on aspects of a mystery story. There is a considerable variety of thought-form to choose from, because devotees have the option of homing in on material lifted from the incarnation which mainly takes their fancy. Nevertheless, in saying this no discouragement of serious service work along the specialized lines of interest known to relate to leadership figureheads is intended. Those who wish to work will not be put off by anything written in a book like this, and we shall doubtless touch more than once on the subject of work-streams aligned to particular lineages.

Another member of the Lodge has been designated by the letter P.[49] When one can read that the character in question occupies an Irish body and has in the past resided in North America, it is all too easy to call him Patrick; and in no time at all it would be possible to have a stray thought-form giving a 'Barry Fitzgerald' performance all over the ethers. This business of naming with letters is, I am afraid, rather like the numbering of acupuncture points prevalent in the West. Dr Hiroshi Motoyama, in a lecture given in London, suggested that this form of Western tidiness sometimes veiled the finer nuances of Eastern therapeutic teaching. In the older, more poetic style of naming, an acupuncture point called 'heavy gate', for instance, gave the practitioner a hint of its quality and function. The pseudonyms adopted for some of the Masters around the turn of the century, such as the Egyptian, the Venetian and so on, seem hardly appropriate to those working in a world context and with planetary concerns. Perhaps such names belong to the type of titling favoured by interior decorators of another era that spoke of 'the Chinese drawing-room', 'the beige bedroom', etc., a style that is no doubt perfectly accurate and quite evocative at its particular level of appeal but one that has gone somewhat out of fashion. When we are a little more aware of the Lodge members as channels for various creative and energetic world work-streams, we may find more adequate nomenclature. Meantime; 'A rose by any other name would smell as sweet.'

What seems to me to be an entirely legitimate attempt to gain a new perspective is the sort of research now being attempted by the authoress Jean Overton-Fuller (of *Madeleine* fame). I hope I do not embarrass Miss Overton-Fuller by mentioning her work in this type of context, for she adopts the role of historian and literary researcher and has based her recent books on an analysis of the documentary material that she is actually able to uncover. In 1981, having worked on her material since 1967, she published a biography of Francis Bacon, [50] who, in A.A.B.'s account was allegedly an incarnation of the Rakoczi consciousness [51] (although Miss Overton-Fuller does not confuse the approach to her material — or her readers — by any such suggestion). She plans to follow this with a study of *Rakoczy and Saint-Germain*, and has managed to find documents and letters undiscovered at the time of Mrs Cooper-Oakley's earlier attempt to make an historical appraisal of this character. A.A.B. makes a fair number of references to R. as her writing unfolds, and in her earliest description of him she confirms that he is mentioned in old historical books. [52] No doubt there will be those who would wish to debate Miss Overton-Fuller's interpretation of her material, but her attempt as a historian to produce these books in tandem is, I think, a courageous one.

The Tibetan Buddhist system of thought is quite used to accepting the idea of a lineage of consciousness with a continuity of incarnations representing an emanation of different aspects of the being. This may well seem strange to the Western hemisphere-trained mind, with its emphasis on individual personality, but can we be sure, if we have any opinion on such matters, that either they or we have got it absolutely right? It could be interesting to look at the development of a unit of consciousness operating through a chain of different personalities in an ongoing history. Such life-by-life biographies may turn out to be modern man's answer to the three-volume novel of Victorian days — publishers prepare!

There was an occasion when a student prepared a picture — quite well painted in oils, I believe — and started to circulate copies of it. A.A.B. was forthright in her comment. I remember finding an old copy of the circular letter which she had sent out at the time. 'A person' she wrote (a crushing description, coming from someone brought up in the Edwardian era), 'was circulating a picture of a Tibetan. It might be a Tibetan, it was not the Tibetan [she knew]'. And that was that. I mention this because of the vexed and paradoxical question of pictures of members of the Lodge and the formal descriptions of individual masters which were circulated through general theosophical channels, in addition to those relayed in A.A.B.'s own books. I have read in a biography of Madame Blavatsky that she instructed a portrait artist who received impressions of some of the identities associated with the Lodge and who were interested in the theosophical movement. Pictures were then painted of them and subsequently passed by Blavatsky. The esoteric section of the Theosophical Society used these pictures in their work, and it was in this context that A.A.B. was able to identify her own contact, thus indicating that the picture must have had a recognizable likeness to the teacher she met when she was fifteen. As she is not the only case I have known of a person identifying a hierarchical contact (a different one from A.A.B.) in this way, the subject seems worth mentioning. A Miss Jacobs, who had been a pupil of Madame Blavatsky, passed on to A.A.B. the photographic plates of these portraits which had been given to her by Colonel Olcott, Madame Blavatsky's co-worker. [53]

These pictures have of course been publicized in a number of books, including, I believe, the Theosophical edition of Manly Palmer Hall's *Secret Teachings of All Ages*, brought out by the Philosophical Research Society. They are not employed by those in the Lucis Trust, an organization (to be discussed later) responsible for carrying on some of the public activities started by A.A.B. Their attitude, as I understand it, is that the essence and energy of the work itself is not dependent on the outer appearance of any individual, and secondly that whoever may be a means of focus for world service of any kind acts as a vortex of energy and inspiration, and it is thus relatively unimportant whether they look like the back end of a bus or a particular oil painting. The principle of impermanence in the world of forms also presumes certain natural changes. D.K.'s remarks on the subject were unequivocal when he wrote, as indicated previously:

The work of the Masters and their freedom to serve humanity as They desire have been greatly hindered by these foolish thought-forms and by the preconceived ideas of well-intentioned aspirants. The Masters very seldom resemble the theories, the pictures and the information which is so frequently circulated by the average aspirant.

Nonetheless, some of us are 'average aspirants' and find that some sort of picture anchors the 'reality' (which was presumably the concern in providing pictures in the first place) of what they inwardly sense or experience. If only in the psychological sense, such emblems can act as points of recollection, though there are those who believe that a properly consecrated or revered object may connect with its principal in somewhat the same way as a radionic practitioner will use a morsel of hair or a drop of blood to experience a vibratory connection with the parent body from which it came. Readers will appreciate that such analogy is always approximate and ultimately unsatisfactory; it is simply a side doorway into a difficult area of thinking and research. Some advice D.K. gave on *The Use of the Lord's Image* includes the statement: 'There is no true image of Him because it must be upon our own hearts and not upon our canvases'. [54] He then begins immediately to comment on the value of a group approach: 'He can and will work through all groups just in so far as they fit themselves for planned service, for the distribution of love, and come into conscious alignment with the greater potency of the inner groups.'

Some lines of group service work which have, at one time or another, attracted hierarchical attention or even been initiated by the Lodge, are recorded by Alice Bailey. Whether one decides to research the material for oneself is a matter of personal option. In any event, the advice in the Christian New Testament 'By their fruits ye shall know them' is entirely appropriate, and deserves re-proclamation. Of obvious interest are the means and methods whereby 'fruitage' comes about. One of A.A.B.'s slimmer volumes — a mere hundred and ninety-seven pages, which is nothing by her standards of productivity — called *Telepathy and the Etheric Vehicle* discusses what the text calls 'the supreme science of contact'. [55] This includes the ability of one level of spiritual consciousness to impress another level with some chosen concept. Whether the concept then works out into manifestation truthfully and gets clothed accurately in mental, emotional and physical substance (should it be something that requires anchoring on the physical plane and in concrete form) is another matter.

However, in the idea of 'Each one teach one', which was a phrase often used by the mystic Frank Laubach in his world literacy campaign, it is possible to see why the Lodge under discussion is frequently referred to as a creative Hierarchy. It is like an outwardly radiating chain of communicating relationships stretching through the dimensions of consciousness. Nowadays one popular image is that of a network along whose grid enlightened ideas can pass into manifestation, emerging from the deepest levels of awareness to blossom beside the most mundane.

A story is related in the book on telepathy just mentioned, to which, of course, the reader is at liberty to apply Foster Bailey's dictum, 'Interesting, if true':

An illustration of this is to be found in the history of the League of Nations. Before He took up special work, the Master Seraphis sought to bring through some constructive idea for the helping of humanity. He conceived of a world unity in the realm of politics which would work out as an intelligent banding of the nations for the preservation of international peace. He presented it to the adepts in conclave and it was felt that something could be done. The Master Jesus undertook to present it to His group of disciples as He was working in the occident. One of these disciples on the inner planes, seized upon the suggestion and passed it on (or rather stepped it down) until it registered in the brain of Colonel House. He, not recording the source (of which he was totally unaware), passed it on in turn to that sixth ray aspirant, Woodrow Wilson. Then, fed by the wealth of analogous ideas in the minds of many, it was presented to the world. It should be borne in mind that the function of a disciple is to focus a stream of energy of some special kind upon the physical plane where it can become an attractive centre of force and draw to itself similar types of ideas and thought currents which are not strong enough to live by themselves or to make a sufficiently strong impact upon the human consciousness. [56]

As we know, in spite of so much effort by so many the League in its original form failed to prevent renewed hostility and broke up. However, it could be said that the initiating concept reincarnated in the United Nations Organization. Who can tell what mutations may eventually befall that instrument under the pressures of human usage? Such speculation is among the subjects considered in a recent book written about the organization by Donald Keys, called *Earth at Omega*. Maybe the story of Seraphis' aid is too fantastical for some. How can we be sure it is true? We cannot. Neither can we be sure it is not, though prejudice may urge disbelief. The important point for us is that we now have a United Nations Organization, an imperfect agency in an imperfect world. It is our responsibility to make it better, if we are up to the task.

A point of significance in the whole idea of this kind of filtering through of vision in whatever aspect of the good, the true and the beautiful may be adopted by its emissaries is the factor of levels or planes of conscious being. To quote again from some of A.A.B.'s material:

From the angle of the old teaching, the Ashram (spiritual group) of the Master and the focus of the Hierarchy were on the higher levels of the mental plane. Today, that is not so. They are on the plane of spiritual love, of the intuition and of buddhi. The Hierarchy is both retreating towards the higher centre of Shamballa, and at the same time advancing towards the lower centre, Humanity. [57]

Although this may seem a somewhat technical explanation, there is nothing in it that conflicts with the orthodox beliefs that the Buddha nature resides in all, that the Christ spirit is within us ('the hope of Glory', as it has been termed by St. Paul) or with the various other expressions of the same truth. This factor of the different levels or areas through which consciousness can operate is bound to keep cropping up — it cannot be avoided — but I shall try to deal with it in reasonably digestible doses. It would seem that, like compelling godparents, the Lodge's Members evoke our climb towards their abiding place by awakening that which is synchronous within ourselves, rather in the way that a parent summons a small child to walk unaided across a room, knowing that the ability to take the needed steps is there potentially.

In respect of what is quoted above, the title used for this chapter is rather like one of the poetic-sounding labels used in ancient acupuncture practice: it is in fact taken from the phraseology of Tibetan Buddhism. It seemed to me an entirely appropriate label for the totality of that energetic organism described by the words 'Spiritual Hierarchy'. In his efforts to communicate a better understanding of this state, D.K. pointed out that, like any organism in nature, including the human race, the Hierarchy is itself open to growth and development:

The forty-nine Ashrams which constitute the Hierarchy in this planetary period are some of them fully active; some are in process of formation, and some are, as yet, in a totally embryonic condition, awaiting the 'focusing ability' of some initiate who is today preparing for the fifth initiation. Essentially and potentially all the Ashrams are equal, and their quality is not competitive; all of them differ as to their planned activity — an activity which is all part of a carefully formulated hierarchical activity. This you need most carefully to remember. The devotion of a disciple to some particular Master is of no importance to that Master or His ashramic group. It is not devotion or predilection or any personality choice which governs the formation of a Master's group. It is ancient relationships, the ability to demonstrate certain aspects of life to demanding humanity and a definite ray expression of quality which determines the hierarchical placement of aspirants in an Ashram. This will perhaps be a new thought to you and is responsible for the reason why A.A.B. has never emphasized concentration on some one of the known Masters. She has always been aware that each central Ashram has associated with it six other Ashrams which are steadily and constantly being organized to meet planetary need. You will note that I did not say 'human need', for the needs of the planet which the Hierarchy has to meet embrace more than those of the fourth kingdom in nature. I would have you ponder these points.[58]

The impression created is that of a finely organized way station in consciousness, balanced between spirit and matter and partaking of both. One can appreciate the need to explain such an organism in terms of energy and synthesis and also the reason for the basically hylozoistic standpoint of many efforts to propound the ageless wisdom.

Gary Zukav made a pertinent and interesting observation in his book *The Dancing Wu Li Masters* (subtitled 'An Overview of the New Physics'), when he wrote:

Some biologists believe that a single plant cell carries within it the capability to reproduce the entire plant. Similarly, the philosophical implication of quantum mechanics is that all of the things in our universe (including us) that appear to exist independently are actually parts of one all-embracing organic pattern, and that no parts of that pattern are ever really separate from it or from each other.[59]

For me this echoes the concept of Hierarchy, and also reflects the many modern efforts to see life and its activities from a holistic viewpoint.

Such concepts, when further researched and understood, may in time lead us to some comprehension of the technical basis for telepathic communication; though, D.K.'s practice of opening up fresh horizons could not always be said to do that. He writes, for example: 'The moment that man *tries* to be telepathic, he is immediately swept into a vortex of abstract energies which condition him for spiritual impression far more than they fit him for personal relationships telepathically established.'[60] Perhaps this accounts in some measure for the impressionability, or suggestibility as the case may be, of groups of people focused in concert on a particular theme and explains why in A.A.B.'s efforts on behalf of human welfare so great an emphasis is laid on impersonal work performed through groups of dedicated people. On occasion abstract concepts can be set loose in groups in a curiously easy way. And I have sometimes heard individuals remark that they have grapsed some point more easily while in a group situation — in a lecture, workshop, class or what have you — than they did while struggling on their own, even though the participation of the group in question may have appeared relatively passive.

Notwithstanding this, A.A.B. seems to have been a telepath in a fairly wide sense, although there is no record of her having taken part in any mechanical Zenner card-type experiments. Her work as D.K.'s amanuensis was not the only instance of her ability for accurate subjective contact: one close woman friend had a fairly marked degree of telepathic exchange with her.[61] A.A.B. herself gave an account of an incident where she fell ill during a European trip her friend immediately became aware of the fact and, being well off, cabled funds without any request, thereby demonstrating the extreme practicality of the ability. A.A.B. also stated that the contact remained after her friend's death and that items of ordinary, down-to-earth information concerning this lady's family would be discussed between them prior to A.A.B. being able to verify the facts at a physical level — an idea which may well seem alarming to all those who have said in fervour, sorrow or hope: 'I trust old So-and-so cannot see what is going on now.' (Ah well, I suppose we all have to learn detachment at some stage in the proceedings!)

One of the key statements in the telepathy book, which a quick flip through its pages reveals repeatedly, is that success at registering impressions of a spiritual nature relies on 'engendering a magnetic aura on which the highest impressions can play'. For some the term 'aura' is fairly vague, and though accepted as part of our general language, it is often applied to that kind of energy which is of a largely emotional nature. However, let us entertain the concept revealed in Dr Harold Saxton Burr's rigorously experimented research into electrodynamic life-fields:

The Universe in which we find ourselves and from which we can not be separated is a place of Law and Order. It is not an accident, nor chaos. It is organised and maintained by an Electro-dynamic Field capable of determining the position and movement of all charged particles.[62]

If we now apply this concept along with Dr Burr's tentative consideration of similar fields at the level of thought — of the 'noosphere', as Teilhard de Chardin spoke of it — to the term 'aura', we begin to have a new working hypothesis.

The art of spiritual impression may seem an abstruse subject and irritatingly vague to our workaday logic, but it has a significant place in any serious consideration of the work of Alice Bailey. This is especially so when operations would appear to be conducted from a level at which the normal sense apparatuses known to us are reportedly in abeyance (as described in the lines quoted earlier from *King John*). Furthermore, this form of communication by impression involves important issues of mental freedom versus totalitarian control. An impression is like a hint: it can be accepted or rejected at will. It can be analysed by common sense and easily ignored altogether in a way that may be difficult where organizational types of instruction, command or even direct and forceful suggestion, whether overt or subliminal, by a strong individual are concerned. Moreover, it allows any group or individual thus impressed to make the concept or objective their own. They then work it out in their own way because they see the purpose of it as worthwhile for its own sake and not merely because a particular authority figure told them it was necessary.

Of course, no method of communication is foolproof as far as human folly is concerned, and hiccups can arise when any one person or group takes an impression as being their very own and theirs alone. It is sometimes noticeable that certain inventions come to a point of fruition almost simultaneously in several different places. Interestingly enough, the same principle may operate through slightly varied systems of mechanism, as I believe — my mother's cousin, Baird, being one of the participants in that precipitation — was the case with television. (Perhaps in the future, close co-operation with the interior groups may obviate a vulgar scramble for the Patent Office.) In the case of television, D.K. remarked through A.A.B., it became easier to externalize as the Masters within the Lodge developed a parallel ability within their own capacity for communication. [63]

Yet, in spite of the old Hindu myth of the nine invisible men [64] perpetually writing and then rewriting the books of human life, I do not think anyone is suggesting that all significant impressions come from a handful of wise adepts and their attendant groups. There is no suggestion in A.A.B.'s writings that we are dealing with Superman or 'Bionic Woman'. The Masters of the Lodge she spoke of are not operating from a point of deified omnipotence, nor are they ever depicted as masters of sorcery or manipulation but only as lords of compassion or masters of wisdom who have progressed a bit further than some of us have in terms of handling themselves and finding out what life may be all about; they then, because of their experience, do what they can to make the way clear and to speed others on the journey. Nevertheless, they cannot take the needed steps for us or remove the birthright of freewill on which our individual guarantee of achievement must be based. Foster Bailey's reply to a question I asked him in the 1950s on how the Masters reached their point of elevation was much the same as an exchange reported between Al Huang and Gary Zukav in the 1970s, though perhaps a shade less poetic. [65] 'They got started sooner,' Foster quipped, — or did he say 'quicker'?

If we are not dealing with Superman, then neither are we dealing with that state of Gods-in-paradise sometimes depicted in religious systems of thought. Such locations may be a temporary resting place, but are reported ultimately just another pocket in consciousness that can delay the spirit from reaching complete liberation. The Masters are seen by A.A.B. as 'having turned back to serve and save'. In several places where accounts of the Lodge's constitution and its early history are discussed, it is pointed out that the hierarchical personnel, like D.K.'s English, improved with time and effort:

In the early days of the Hierarchy, millenia of years ago, neither the official Directors of the Hierarchy nor the Masters were of the calibre which They are today. Had They been so, They would have been too far removed from the factual life of the cycle, and therefore useless for the cycle of divine life which existed. The growth of humanity and its evolutionary status (when compared with primordial and primitive man) can be seen in the quality of the Hierarchy today, *which humanity produced* and towards which it looks for guidance and teaching. This is an interesting point which I offer for your consideration. [66]

Perhaps the evocative needs of a speeding world evolution had something to do with it. In fact, the assertion is made [67] that in the dim and distant past the Masters were from another place and returned whence they had come as and when earth's own humanity demonstrated itself up to making it on its own — a legend, myth or approximation of a truth difficult to understand at this point of time. Readers must settle the matter with themselves.

A great deal of what A.A.B. reported seems to reflect a tremendous co-operative drive for world betterment and human liberation, initiated to some extent from within the Lodge. Yet if we look to the mythological record of the past as a means of deducing the behaviour of such subliminal factors in former times, it is intriguing to notice that stories of the ancient pantheons of deity as viewed from different cultural locations frequently depict the celestial persons as rather prone to less than amicable debate amongst themselves. A.A.B. now offers, if nothing else, a psychological mythology for a New Age in which integration, synthesis, co-operation, maturity of outlook and a holistic world view are significant factors in the subjective interweaving: a fresh myth that calls on us to grow, along with grown-up gods.

There are many who see myths as valid attempts to visualize the subliminal interplay of variously qualified psychological, psychic and spiritual energies. Joseph Campbell's first and fourth definitions of the function of myth are: 'To evoke and support as sense of awe before the mystery of being' and 'To guide men stage by stage in health, strength and harmony of spirit through the foreseeable stages of a useful life.'[68] Myth is certainly valuable in researching the inner growth and unfolding of the human race because it offers a graphic picture of the forces at work within our being, and this without recourse to any special dogma or school of philosophy.

Using the guidance of the mythological framework, it is possible to sketch in an impression of Djwhal Khul's service function and speculate on his place in the scheme of things. He has been called 'the messenger of the Masters', not merely because of his work with Madame Blavatsky and Alice Bailey in making a public presentation of the teachings of the ageless wisdom but because of his reputation for taking on whatever had to be done.[69] Thus speaking in terms of *mythological function*, one can visualize him in the position of a nuncio for the messenger Mercury, a prototype of the enlightener Hermes or of the magical scribe, Thoth; and if one wishes to expand the speculation more basically, Loge, who was 'Mr Fixit' for the Nordic gods, is also present (all these mythological characters being, as it were, counterparts of each other, within the cultures from which they received their clothing). Maybe the Masters of whom Alice Bailey spoke represent, to some degree, archetypal vortices of energy. Psychologically and philosophically, we can ponder on the function of the energy and learn to work with it. Certainly, as far as human aspirants to the mysteries are concerned, D.K. can be seen acting through A.A.B.'s writings in the Hermetic role of 'guardian of crossroads and borderlands', a task traditionally assigned to Mercury.

However, I dare say not too much should be made of the mythological function of any particular member of the Lodge, even though it is a relevant consideration when it comes to understanding their work. Myths have gathered their energy over very great periods of time; moreover, they probably do veil deep psychological and psychic currents, as is supposed. They are definitely one of the ways in which we can learn to understand our ancient conditioning. It is also wise to recall that Carl Jung advised wrestling with archetypes, just as Jacob wrestled with his angel and Castaneda with his 'ally', so that we may come to know the force within them through the fully rounded strength of our own humanity. No one, I suspect, wishes to be absorbed wholesale, like some undistinguished protoplasmic lump, into the fabric of a fantasy.

If D.K. seems to be cast in the role of Hermetic oracle, with A.A.B. as Delphic servant, then Foster Bailey played the long-suffering production manager who got the whole show on the road and kept it there. He often joked that there had been two or three people before him on the Master's short list of possible assistants for A.A.B.'s public effort. He relates that when he asked her to marry him they were looking onto a field containing a horse. 'If the horse nods, I suppose I'd better,' or words to that effect, was the lady's alleged reply. The animal having given its instant assent, they got married one day in the lunch hour and then went back to their office. It was a highly successful partnership, carried forward in love and service, and in a very real sense Foster Bailey made much of the work his own. An American attorney and air force pilot, he had become an officer of the Theosophical Society and was at Krotona, the Californian headquarters of the Society and its esoteric section in America, when Alice Evans went to live and work there. As she commenced her writing, there was — perhaps inevitably, as it is such a common pattern of events — organizational reaction, although it was actually over matters concerning the running of the Society and the freedom of participation of its members that public debate broke out.

The redoubtable Mrs Annie Besant, who had done so much for the Theosophical movement, was then the elderly head of the Society and could only be reached in India by letter or cable, though she did send a representative over at some point. Again perhaps inevitably (those familiar with the development of groups will recognize how often the young seed must fall right away from the parent plant in order to grow properly), after various meetings and discussions, Alice and Foster Bailey began working independently of the Theosophical Society and set up operations in New York; although, I believe, for many years A.A.B. continued as a dues-paying member and Foster Bailey acted as secretary to an independent theosophical association in New York City. Also inevitable, however, is the speculation (within *Lob's Garden*[70]) on how things might have turned out if A.A.B.'s work had grown up within the mainstream of The Theosophical Society's organization.

Mrs Besant seems to have been a peripheral figure in the story, and I can find no account of her having met the Baileys; A.A.B.'s period in India as a young woman took place long before Mrs Besant's ascendancy as Theosophical Society World President. Admired by many for her early reforming work with the match girls' strike, she was by all accounts a dynamic figure, drawing large numbers through her public lecture work and published books. *A Study in Consciousness* was much admired by A.A.B. Nevertheless, in the style of the times, Mrs Besant seems to have been a fairly autocratic leader.[71] During the 1914-18 war she was already involved in Indian political life. Another (related) John Sinclair, First Baron Pentland of Lyth, was the British Governor in Madras, where the Theosophical Society world headquarters are situated at Adyar. He had the unenviable task of placing Mrs Besant under restraint when it became impossible to modify the virulent style of attack with which she chose to forward the Home Rule for India campaign to the detriment of the Allied war effort. John Pentland was himself a popular and socially aware politician (he had, incidentally, studied A. P. Sinnett's *Esoteric Buddhism*), who had conceived and piloted Scottish land reform through both Houses of the British Parliament, after which Asquith asked him to serve overseas. He was at the time much vilified by the theosophists, but due to his impersonality and legendary reticence in relation to his personal concerns, he said not a word in his own defence. [72]

I mention this incident — which must appear to have nothing to do with Alice Bailey's story — not just to set the record straight on past history and certainly not to criticize either of the principals, but because this is a small yet striking instance of a familiar pattern of human behaviour which frequently has to be offset. It is an example of 'warfare in heaven' and has great relevance to the evolution of groups. For here we have an occasion where two individuals, both, if we can make an assessment from the bulk of their public work, on the side of the angels, found themselves in a situation where they had to make life difficult for each other: the firebrand with prevision of an idea *before* its time had come and the public official who had to react within the context of a larger, global picture and the need of more immediate and pressing objectives. One saddening form of infighting is violent tactical argument among world servers, which resembles the behaviour of the 'Old Age' mythical gods, with all their bickering. The bitter conflicts between science and religion, for example, both seeking the enlightenment of mankind, could, with a little more knowledge on both sides and a modicum of goodwill, fade into obscurity. The very special effort made by D.K. and the Baileys to awaken men and women of goodwill to united, intelligent and constructive action, even while concentrating on their own chosen lines of specialization, is a major part of this theme.

If we can at least consider the idea of a united, inner Lodge trying to prepare the way, then perhaps we can take with us the possibility of many outer groups responding to synthesizing impression from within. D.K.'s prospect [73] of inner, transcendent, subjective groups can be visualized as work-guilds, creative ashrams or spiritual households, all related within the one inconceivable Mansion. Each of them pursues its dharma duty through the centuries, growing and expanding as its work unfolds, coming forward to activity or retiring quietly, as the qualified energies to which its specialization responds, cycle in and out of manifestation. The vision is one of a veritable cosmic dance of waxing and waning lights, of groups passing the task of world succour from one to another as they blend their forces in an invisible tapestry of purpose. What if the overseeing Mansion of Perception should now meld and fuse the many efforts in some new way, so that the component lights should harmonize and coalesce in laser-like intensity? We will consider the possibility, as Alice Bailey saw it, as we go along.

One final incident will serve to close this chapter. An old friend told me of an incident at A.A.B.'s English home when someone, incredulous of Masters of wisdom, demanded to know in all honesty whether they really existed. 'Oh yes,' said Mrs Bailey quietly, adding after a slight pause, 'and they are beautiful.'

In a pamphlet A.A.B. quoted a favourite passage of Robert Browning's verse:

> . . . For men begin to pass their nature's bound,
> And find new hopes and cares which fast supplant
> Their proper joys and griefs; they grow too great
> For narrow creeds of right and wrong; which fade
> Before the unmeasured thirst for good; while peace
> Rises within them ever more and more.
> Such men are even now upon the earth,
> Serene amid the half-formed creatures round
> Who should be saved by them and joined with them.

2. 'A Governess for Saints'?

In the course of her work as a journalist, Annie Besant, I recall hearing, was sent a copy of Madame Blavatsky's *The Secret Doctrine* to review. That book, so difficult and so extraordinary to some, was to her a natural expression of ideas that were of the greatest relevance to her own thinking. In a word, she took to it, sought the author out and made the cause of theosophy her own. While the outer circumstances were quite different, Alice Bailey, it appears, also took to it. And it was not long after she had joined the theosophical lodge in Pacific Grove, California that she herself was giving classes based on *The Secret Doctrine*[1]; although she records that when, having stabilized her finances a little, she moved to the theosophical headquarters at Krotona in Hollywood, one of her first duties was emptying garbage cans for the cafeteria. She later took on the cooking.[2]

Later still, in 1921, and once the Baileys had moved to New York, A.A.B. started a *Secret Doctrine* class which was well attended, with students coming in from a number of different groups. And from these classes, originally held in a location on Madison Avenue, groups in other American cities first received the outline lessons by post.[3] The period 1920-23 seems to have been a cycle of important anchoring work in preparation for A.A.B.'s later service. The books *Initiation, Human and Solar, Letters on Occult Meditation* and *Consciousness of the Atom* (this last based on some of her own lectures) all appeared at this time. And as a result of these publications she began to get letters from all over the world. In 1921 a group of five men would assemble on Tuesdays after office hours to meditate with Alice and Foster Bailey; when, a year later, the Baileys went to Long Island for a three-month stay, A.A.B. undertook to write a weekly letter to this group. This letter on spiritual subjects sometimes seemed an appropriate reply to one of the enquiries that arrived through the mail.

This looked like a spontaneous and natural response to expressed need. However, by the time the Baileys returned to New York in September 1922 they had to consider seriously the best way in which to meet the ever-increasing demands for *Secret Doctrine* class work and the numerous appeals for spiritual advice. In April 1923 and with the help of the Tuesday group they set about establishing the Arcane School as a channel through which serious enquirers could be offered lessons by correspondence.[4] Only one of this original group had ever belonged to a correspondence school, but they all had a burning desire to be of assistance to sincere enquirers. And since those days, many tens of thousands of students world-wide have passed through the school, and the work has developed and been translated into a fair number of languages.

In 1950, after A.A.B.'s death, in an address to some of the school's students assembled in New York, Foster Bailey indicated[5] that the plan to set up a school whose pupils could learn the principles of the ageless wisdom, develop the quality of soul within their lives and start to aid the plans for world salvage to which the inner Lodge was committed had all been implanted in A.A.B.'s deep consciousness prior to her incarnation on the physical stage. It has often been speculated that certain individuals have work they seem destined to carry forward; the suggestion a free-will decision has been made at another level of consciousness and of time puts an interesting perspective on this possibility. In any case, realizing such good intentions and anchoring them in a practical and effective way was the particular basic challenge that A.A.B. set herself in terms of personal service. Many may have such deeply laid plans, but few manage to work them through so that they come to abundant fruition.

I have heard that A.A.B. maintained that a common dictionary was one of the world's most esoteric books because it gave people entry to the world of meaning. Working on that tack, the word 'arcane', used as a title for the school she started, simply means: 'hidden, occult, esoteric, a mystery'. In some senses, possibly an alchemical use, *'arcanum'* can mean an elixir and is therefore a symbol of hope. As a matter of fact, A.A.B. learnt that Madame Blavatsky had at one time intended to call the esoteric section of the Theosophical Society the Arcane School, and decided in her own work that 'the old lady should have her wish'.[6] This perhaps indicates how closely A.A.B. felt herself, at that time, identified with the mainsprings of the modern theosophical movement, although the subsequent development of her own work also indicated just how far and how wide the vision drawn through that movement could spread in world service.

When we consider the sheer physical weight of the books produced by A.A.B., it seems remarkable by any standards that she also managed to bring up a family on a shoestring and run an international correspondence school, as well as carrying out public lecture work and other activities, some of which will be discussed in subsequent pages. By the end of the 1920s, the response to her intense activity reportedly had her secretary fixing interviews for people wishing to see her at twenty-minute intervals throughout the day.[7] All this was just part and parcel of her public or exoteric work; behind that there was the interior or esoteric activity with the inner family of which she was a part and whose influence radiated from the one who had come to remind her in childhood about her planned intention.

Nonetheless, the effort does not appear to have been in any way magical or mysterious in its accomplishment simply the result of very hard, highly organized work. Towards the end of her life she admitted to feeling extremely tired.[8] The discipline of achievement had been laid while she was young, in a Victorian nursery regime — a regime against which many of today's Western children would simply come out in revolt.[9] A.A.B. and her sister used to rise at six, starting the day with preparatory work for lessons, piano practice or both. Schoolroom breakfast was at eight o'clock sharp before family prayers in the big dining-room downstairs at nine. Formal lessons with a governess began half an hour later. There was a recreation period morning and afternoon for a walk, outing or other form of exercise, and an hour's rest on a flat sloping board while their governess read them an improving book. At five in the afternoon they would be despatched to the family drawing-room, appropriately dressed if guests were staying; there they were inspected until fetched by the governess. (A.A.B. appears to have looked on this as a moment of rescue.) Supper was at six-thirty, followed by more lessons until bedtime at eight. There were, needless to say, rules about everything.

This was the somewhat regimented schedule at her

Moor Park (pictured in a 1912 sale catalogue), the house where Alice Bailey spent childhood years with her La Trobe-Bateman grand-parents.

grandparents' home, where A.A.B. and her sister were brought up after consumption had caused the death of their mother and subsequently that of their father. Her grandfather was John Frederic La Trobe-Bateman, a well-known engineer responsible for, among other things, a number of municipal water systems in Great Britain. [10] His home, where she spent a great deal of the period between seven and thirteen years of age, was Moor Park in Surrey. A fine Queen Anne English country house built by Sir William Temple, it was one of those chosen by Josiah Wedgwood as a decoration for the great dinner service commissioned from him by Catherine the Great of Russia and now to be seen among the art treasures of Leningrad's Hermitage museum. The house has been an adult education centre run by the local authority, but is, I understand, once more for sale. One of A.A.B.'s final memories of it before the family sold it after La Trobe-Bateman's death was of her grandfather's coffin in state there, surmounted by one huge wreath sent by Queen Victoria.

Whatever else A.A.B. may have learnt from her childhood regime, she was certainly indoctrinated with the habit of work. She also maintained later that a doctor told her that she was one of those who could manage on relatively little sleep; somewhere around four hours a night was the alleged figure.

It is sometimes to be noted in spiritual experience that at various stages on the way the traveller meets those who act as sponsors, companions or tutors, call them what you will. There does not appear to be anything formal or outwardly arranged in this, and it is not a business of finding a guru: certain key individuals just emerge in the course of the subject's life and, regardless of their function in relation to outer events, demonstrate an ability to speak to his soul. A.A.B. goes on record [11] as recognizing the paramount influences of a governess, Miss Godby, to whom she seems to have been fairly obnoxious as a young girl, and of her aunt, Margaret Maxwell, whose Scottish home she sometimes visited. Both gave her stability and a sense of real values and therefore stood by her as spiritual sponsors, making possible her subsequent entry into fuller work for the Lodge.

It is in large measure through its implantation of a sense of values — values to live by — that the work of the Arcane School can be assessed. Initially, it could be said that the school curriculum aims to awaken in its students an esoteric sense of what life could be all about. In *A Treatise on White Magic* we find a discussion (which we will write about more fully later on) wherein the particularly fine quality of inner awareness aimed for in world servers is described quite precisely:

In the gathering together in the world at this time (first published in 1934) of the New Group of World Servers, true caution must be preserved. Each worker is responsible for himself and for his service and for no one else. It is wise to gauge and approximate the evolutionary status, not upon claims made, but upon work accomplished and the love and wisdom shown. Judgement should be based upon an evidenced knowledge of the plan as it works out in the wise formulation of the next step ahead for the human race; upon a *manifested esoteric sense*, and upon an influence or an auric power which is wide, constructive and inclusive.

You ask me to define more clearly what I mean by the words 'esoteric sense'. I mean essentially the power to live and to function subjectively, to possess a constant inner contact with the soul and the world in which it is found, and this must work out subjectively through love, actively shown; through wisdom, steadily outpoured; and through that capacity to include and identify oneself with all that breathes and feels which is the outstanding characteristic of all truly functioning sons of God. I mean, therefore, an interiorly held attitude of mind which can orient itself at will in any direction.[12]

It was apparently Alice Bailey's objective to swell the ranks of, and the support given for, selfless world workers of many kinds, and also to awaken an esoteric sense of consciousness that could manifest itself creatively and beneficiently for this purpose.

On approaching the school an applicant receives a paper discussing what an esoteric school is for, in terms of the sort of material just quoted. It is up to the would-be student to make the approach: in tune with masonic practice, the school neither solicits custom nor seeks advertising. Plenty of people — and their number increases as time goes by — know of the school's existence. These may or may not discuss it among their own contacts, but there is nothing to be gained by getting individuals to take part in work of this nature if it cannot engage the heart's attention; they have got to want to undertake it very much indeed. All along the way, effort is self-initiated, and this seems to reflect a great principle of life. If applicants go forward after satisfying themselves and the school on this point, and if they make a start with the work, three main related lines of activity will engage their attention: meditation, study and service.

First and foremost is meditation, because this, as D.K. puts it, 'is the means par excellence for building "the new man in Christ" '.[13] Meditation is an inborn human ability, like breathing, which can awaken consciousness to its full estate. A huge number of books and classes are now available discussing different styles and techniques for developing this natural ability; this book is not one of these volumes. Meditative work of an occult nature, employing visualization and other natural faculties, is nevertheless an integral part of the school's programme.

Secondly, there is study. This concerns the development of the mind's contents. Many of the aspirants who first approached A.A.B. having read her books or heard her lectures experienced a strong degree of emotional response to what they heard. This was all very well in its way, yet a steady mental polarization was what was really required for sustained creative work. Someone asking me about the Arcane School said he had heard that students sat exams and 'that sort of thing'. Certainly, a number of written papers are required so that concepts and musings do not remain vague and inchoate but have to be thought through by students and anchored by them in their own words.

Finally there is the question of service. This is another essential part of the threefold activity of the school, though it is something that requires a personal decision and is an aspect of the programme that each student must work out for himself. Yet as new energy comes into play within people it is important that it should find a constructive and creative outlet — otherwise, what is the whole effort for? It is not enough that it is intended to be life-enhancing; it has to be demonstrated as such. And that, if you like, seems to be the real 'exam' that the school work inevitably sets up, though it is one that is in the control of the individual student at all times.

The point is made right from the start that the student of the esoteric sense of life is inevitably self-taught. Each life situation is the classroom, and every relationship is the teacher. Once this open approach is grasped, the school can be seen as an association of fellow students rather than as any kind of 'them' teaching 'us' or 'us' teaching 'them'. In this sense the school staff serve as a sort of postbox and sorting office, because one of the things which A.A.B. built into the fabric of her school was the requirement of impersonality. The experience she had had of theosophical politicking and her awareness of the many feuds and factions that can bedevil even the best-intentioned, most altruistic of groups made her determined to emphasize spiritual impersonality so that individuals would learn to look behind first appearances. The cult of personality was anathema to her and remains so to those carrying on the work she began through the Arcane School.

While particular people have had to take responsibility in relation to specific functions, emphasis is not placed on the position held. Students are given individual attention with their written papers and make reports on their meditation work through an ingenious network of 'secretaries' or commentators. Laubach's principle 'Each one teach one' is here at work again, because each student is put in contact, through the headquarters office in his region, with another student of longer standing, preferably one in another country so that impersonality is again maintained. This contact is changed from time to time. It is the secretary's task to companion the work, encouraging and drawing out the student's own innate capacities, the real teacher being, as we have indicated, the quality of soul existing within each person. As A.A.B. once tartly remarked when reviewing work standards: 'Some students make progress despite their secretaries.'

This factor of individual responsibility has meant that the work material of the Arcane School has not remained static. A.A.B.'s original weekly letters developed fairly rapidly into comprehensive study papers based on subject matter drawn from a multitude of sources, by no means purely theosophical. The universality of the spiritual path was at all times emphasized, and some of the early papers had a wonderfully eclectic feel to them. However, recent years have seen a huge boom in the publishing of spiritual and metaphysical literature as public demand for it has grown in many countries of the free world. Books that were hard to come by in the 1940s are now readily available in paperback, and the general attitude to meditation and other spiritual considerations has opened up remarkably. Consequently it has been possible to condense and telescope much of the previous work so that individuals can deal with material — which may no longer seem so strange as it once did — at an increased pace. This acceleration is, of course, amplified where students are able to recognize the points and principles emphasized in terms of their own life experience.

At one time the school was organized in a series of degrees corresponding to different levels of work, rather as is sometimes the case with craft lodges. However, it is easy to appreciate that such degrees arose out of the variety of function (speculative or practical) within the wholeness of the work to be done. I would judge that the present dispensation of the school relies more on the potentially descriptive titles (corresponding to the old-style names for acupuncture points) used to cover the different courses within its work, of which one example is 'The Lighted Way of Integration'. This is done to offset any possible sense of false superiority. Advancing through a series of man-made lessons does not confer any spiritual or organizational seniority; such lessons are designed simply to promote that inner growth and maturity which will automatically bring about change in the way an individual approaches his own environment and life opportunities.

A great deal of the school material used nowadays is, I believe, drawn from Djwhal Khul's writings through A.A.B., despite the fact that he played no active part in the formation of the school, which, as we have mentioned, was A.A.B.'s own particular project and responsibility. It is possible to detect elements of Tibetan secret doctrine surfacing in D.K.'s renderings, as in, for example, his advice on the use of the 'sacred word' — the tone sound 'Om' as in 'Om mani padme hum' ('Hail to the jewel in the Lotus') — and the teaching on the causal lotus vehicle itself, used by the soul energy (see Appendix C). Such subject matter may at first glance seem complex, but if it is compared with an account such as that given in Lama Govinda's *Fundamentals of Tibetan Mysticism* or with some of the translations and commentaries made available in the West through Wallas Budge, it is possible to detect an actual simplification of fundamental principles. Besides this there is in D.K.'s version an obvious effort to universalize all the teaching given so that it can be picked up by interested people approaching from any direction.

As the manuscripts left by A.A.B. have now all been published and are increasingly available in a variety of languages, the teaching is available en masse to anyone who cares to pick up a book or two. It has, however, been prepared in digestible packages by the Arcane School and other groups which base their service on the D.K. — A.A.B. writings. This includes the 'antahkarana' ('walking the way and building the bridge') construction work, which is a sort of core endeavour in this type of growth work. Material on this subject is available and is discussed at length in a ninety-page section of the fifth volume of *A Treatise on the Seven Rays (The Rays and the Initiations)*. It is also discussed in a shorter book, *Education in the New Age*, which puts the subject in less esoteric terms than does the former. Nevertheless, it is of considerable significance both to all that we are discussing in this book and to the future growth of the work in general, so we must take a page or two to elaborate on it now.

The word 'antahkarana' reportedly comes from two Sanskrit terms meaning 'inner' and 'instrument'. [14] It is, in the widest sense, literally the science of the spiritual path itself because, as the old adage has it, 'A conscious being walks the path by becoming the path'. In Indian scripture, the spider is sometimes used as a symbol for this fact because it is out of its own substance that the spider spins its thread. [15] Djwhal Khul, among many descriptions that he gave, wrote: 'The Antahkarana is symbolic of the Path; it is the line of living energy which links the various human aspects and the soul; it holds the clue to the Path'. In threading one's way through the various descriptions of the path, it is evident that the building of the antahkarana can be applied to many different technical stages of the evolution of consciousness. The shifting of emphasis from an emotional to a more mentally perceptive attitude to life, which we have already referred to, is just one tiny step. The seeming gap which appears between the human mechanism operating in the worlds of form and the spiritual being in essence (as indicated in the charts given in Appendix C) is another, larger step. And it is one which applies both to the individual and the collective, as is shown in such ancient myths as Richard Wagner used for his music drama *Rhinegold* (Part 1 of the *Ring of the Nibelungen*), where the gods have to employ the dual capacity of the Gods of Light and of Storm to build the Rainbow Bridge from earth across the void to their giant-built home, Valhalla. According to D.K.'s understanding, [16] Christ in the Garden of Gethsemane (when he prayed 'Father, thy will not mine be done' and went forward to his destiny) forged a new strand of the whole world antahkarana.

With regard to the technical construction of this path in consciousness, in a paper on the antahkarana, D.K. wrote: [17]

The bridge then to be built is often called the 'Rainbow Bridge':

a) It is constructed of all the colours of the seven rays. These are light radiations.

b) It is composed of seven strands of energy or of seven streams of force, because the disciple uses all the seven rays.

c) This is possible because in his agelong personality incarnations he has been on all seven rays.

d) The soul ray dominates finally and in the Rainbow Bridge the colour of the disciple's rays are heard vibrating; the note of his ray is seen.

(Therefore, he does not specifically build in the seven colours or strands. This happens automatically — A.A.B.)
(See Appendix B for a comment on the ray energies.)

Madame Blavatsky wrote about the 'antaskarana', as she spelt it, in *The Voice of the Silence*, and in a footnote to A.A.B.'s *A Treatise on Cosmic Fire* referring to this earlier teaching, there is the following quotation:

The antaskarana is the imaginary path between the personal and impersonal self, and is the highway of sensation; it is the battlefield for mastery over the personal self. It is the path of aspiration, and where one longing for goodness exists the antaskarana persists.[18]

The mention of the imagination is in fact extraordinarily important: it gives a hint to the reverse side of the conditioning by 'outside' influence and circumstance which we touched on in the last chapter. For as the transformation and transmutation of man's kama-manasic substance[19] takes place in the alchemy of life experience, so he learns to handle the capacities of imagination more and more creatively. When seen in this light, the words 'It's just imagination', usually no more than a scornful dismissal, take on an entirely different hue. Stop for a moment and consider honestly how much human beings have summoned to themselves through the gateway of the imagination. It is possible to argue that all construction, however elementary and at whatever level, requires an act of imagination to make it possible; and a great deal of that which is destructive, though less perceptive, can make use of this same internal faculty. It was Emile Coué who was attributed with the statement that in an argument between the will and the imagination, the imagination always wins — a point reconsidered in the psychosynthesis work promoted by Dr Roberto Assagioli.[20]

In visioning 'that which is right and which ought to be' (as D.K. sometimes put it)[21] the individual employing esoteric sensibility to evoke and invoke the necessary energy uses creative imagination. This applies to the redecoration of a room, planning a business, reforming a life, or what you will. To bridge the gap between 'earth' and 'Valhalla', between the raw material of now and the vision of what could be, individuals and groups need to awaken sufficient spiritual confidence to act 'as if'. As truth, goodness, or beauty touch the heart or mind with vision, the creative worker starts to act 'as if' it could be so, and that act of identification becomes their emissary and agency. Within the being of the one who works, and out of his or her own substance, comes the bridging energy by which the project arrives at tangibility. This attitude or technique — if that is the right word for it — is woven into the whole teaching on the construction of the antahkarana (although, in writing about it in these few words, I am reducing it to rather simplistic terms).

The whole subject is well attested to in common myths, so perhaps another point of view will help to make the subject clearer. Mircea Eliade discusses it in *Shamanism:*

We here have a mythological complex whose principal constituents would appear to be the following: (a.) in illo tempore, in the paradisal time of humanity, a bridge connected earth with heaven and people passed from one to the other without encountering any obstacles, because there was not yet death; (b.) once the easy communications between earth and heaven were broken off, people could not cross the bridge except 'in spirit', that is, either as dead or in ecstasy; (c.) this crossing is difficult, in other words, it is sown with obstacles . . . (d.) certain privileged persons nevertheless succeed in passing over it during their lifetimes, be it in ecstasy, like shamans, or by 'force' like certain heroes, or finally, 'paradoxically' through 'wisdom' or initiation. [22]

Other echoes of the concept appear throughout spiritual and mystical writings; one example comes from St. John of the Cross: 'This secret wisdom is a ladder on which the soul climbs upward and downward, until it attains to mystical union.' [23] And the famous Christian Biblical statement, attributed to St. Paul, is another: 'Faith is the substance of things hoped for, the evidence of things not seen.' [24]

This appears in several places in the A.A.B.-D.K. writings. The creation of a matrix in which constructive acts can flourish would appear to be the complementary act to creating 'an aura on which the highest impressions can play', as in the practice of the science of impression discussed earlier.

Of course, people hesitate, understandably, at the thought of possible endless 'becoming', at the sheer strength of energy necessary for change; but in fact in its identification with creative human work, consciousness is simply experiencing life. The technical measurement of the here to the there is a momentary, ephemeral thing, necessary in jumping any gap or void. It is just a case of sensible judgement in the practice of what the politician R.A. Butler called 'the art of the possible'. The bridge, like a dendrite in the brain, relates: it joins where formerly there was separation.

As is often pointed out, one of the main facilities available to man in this practice is sound, speech, the instrument of the word, in whatever form it may take from time to time. [25] This theme, too, appears again and again in D.K.'s writings and is exemplified in the written school work which A.A.B.'s project instituted.

The actual development of the teaching as presented through A.A.B.'s school is at once more profound, more detailed and more technical than anything we have touched on here. In actuality, whether in terms of the world or the individual, the inner bridge or antahkarana, as is hinted at in old myths of the thread of destiny, [26] is a three-ply thread. The first strand of this is the *life-stream or thread*, called the 'sutratma' in some interpretations, the core of life energy that gives beingness. It is anchored in the heart or central core of the creature concerned. That aspect of the life-thread referred to as 'ths silver cord'[27] is often noticed in spiritualistic and other accounts of out-of-the-body experiences.[28] However, this functions, as far as human beings are concerned, in an automatic or inherent way. What is of immediate concern to our study and is most usually considered to be the antahkarana building work, as far as this phase of the teaching is concerned, is the second, the *consciousness thread*. This is anchored in the head and relates to awareness and to the development and expansion of consciousness. Through the interaction of these two, and interwoven with them both in order to accomplish the formation of the complete cable, is the final thread, that of *creativity*. This is anchored in the throat, the organ of sound (in terms of psychic energy at least, even though someone might be dumb at the physical level), with subsidiary creative outlets at the hands and feet. These five interacting creative attributes represent a five-pointed star of ascendancy.

Can we see in this interior building work a correspondence or reflection of our earlier statement about the basic learning activity induced by meditation, study and service, under whatever names we may know them? The creative imagination appears to function in this respect as a *modus operandi* between the intangible, transcendent sphere of awareness and the practicalities of the workaday world. It is all a little like the early telephones, which produced their sound by the oscillation of a magnetic coil vibrating between two diaphragms: the oscillation of awareness between the so-called lower and higher manas-mind (see Appendix C) is the antahkarana coming into action. One final word, taken from the A.A.B.-D.K. writings, may evoke fruitful speculation on what could be revealed through the agency of the 'inner instrument':

What must be grasped is that *all that is is ever present*. What we are concerned with is the constant awakening to that which eternally IS, and to what is ever present in the environment but of which the subject is unaware, owing to short-sightedness. The aim must be to overcome the undue concentration upon the foreground of daily life which characterizes most people, the intense preoccupation with the interior states or moods of the lower self which characterizes the spiritually minded people and the aspirants, and the imperviousness or lack of sensitivity which characterizes the mass of men. The Kingdom of God is present on Earth today and forever has been, but only a few, relatively speaking, are aware of its signs and manifestations. The world of subtle phenomena (called formless, because unlike the physical phenomena with which we are so familiar) is ever with us and can be seen and contacted and proved as a field for experiment and experience and activity if the mechanism of perception is developed as it surely can be. The sounds and sights of the heavenly world (as the mystics call it) are as clearly perceived by the higher initiate as are the sights and sounds of the physical plane as you contact it in your daily round of duties. The world of energies, with its stream of directed force and its centres of concentrated light are likewise present, and the eye of the see-er can see it, just as the eye of the mental clairvoyant can see the geometrical pattern which thoughts assume upon the mental plane, or as the lower psychic can contact the glamours, the illusions and delusions of the astral world. The subjective realm is vitally more real than is the objective, once it is entered and known. It is simply (how simple to some and how insuperably difficult to others, apparently!) a question of the acceptance, first of all, of its existence, the development of a mechanism of contact, the cultivation of the ability to use this mechanism at will, and then *inspired interpretation*. [29]

The implications of this passage are obviously many, but it does indicate tides and cycles of subjective energy with which it is perfectly possible for human beings anywhere to co-operate. One fairly straightforward and well-known subtle tide with which the Arcane School encourages experiment and co-operation (though it is of course not alone in doing this) is the lunar cycle. This has led to what has become known — slightly erroneously, it has always seemed to me — as the full-moon meditation work. What is in fact taken advantage of in this periodic opportunity is the run of the solar energy and the subtle beneficent forces which form a part of this. To put the whole picture in the simplest possible terms, at the period of the full moon the earth benefits from the maximum amount of life-enhancing solar energy because the globe of the moon is out of the light and more or less over the other side of our planet, where it can act to some extent as a reflector. Hence this is a time of stretching into the light, both metaphorically and actually: a time of lifting and aspiration, in psychological terms, when spiritual contact with the Lodge is facilitated. To complement this idea with the other aspect of the cycle, the new moon period can equally be a time of planting, precipitation and anchoring in the earth. This cycle and its extremely practical agricultural consequences have been closely considered by Rudolf Steiner. The effect we see in the tides of the sea is an almost physical manifestation of lunar pull; D.K. maintained that tides exist which are more subtle than that.

A correlative parallel can be seen in our own inhalation, with the small interlude at the 'top' of the breath and in our exhalation, a tiny interlude again occurring as the 'tide turns'; in these interludes, things happen. In this example, at the high point, the human brain and blood are effectively oxygenated and the capilliaries free themselves of toxic gases. It is possible that exchanges are also taking place at other levels. The Hermetic principle 'As above so below' embraced by most presentations of the ageless wisdom would suggest that the outer effects only faintly mirror the more subtle and spiritual experience.

The work of meditation and invocation at the time of the full moon is an occasion when Arcane School offices, wherever these may be established, offer the chance of participating in a public service to anyone in sympathy with the objective of these occasions, whether part of the school student group or not. Thus it is that a great many people in different parts of the world hold services and meditation meetings which take advantage of this flow of solar energy, their action either prompted by the school's example or taken on their own initiative but always conducted in an entirely autonomous way. One of the school's brief explanations given in their suggested outline for an invocative meditation (see Appendix D in conjunction with Appendix A) runs as follows:

The time of the full moon is a period when spiritual energies are uniquely available, and facilitate a closer rapport between humanity and the Hierarchy. Each month the inflowing energies carry the specific qualities of the constellation (astrological) influencing the particular month; these energies playing sequentially upon humanity, establish the 'divine attributes' in the consciousness of men . . . Entrance upon the Path of Approach is possible for individuals, for groups and for humanity as a whole, as a unit. Energies not usually or normally contacted can be touched, grasped and utilized at the time of these Approaches, provided that they are contacted in group formation. Thus the individual, the group and humanity, are enriched and vitalized. [30]

An ancient piece of commentary describing what is simultaneously a spiritual opportunity and a chance to work in service within the human world was quoted by D.K. in the course of his work with A.A.B. This passage has become a sort of keynote for the whole network of endeavour at the time of the solar inflow clocked by the full moon.

He who faces the light and stands within its radiance is blinded to the issues of the world of men; he who passes on the Lighted Way to the great Centre of Absorption. But he who feels the urge to pass that way yet loves his brother on the darkened path, revolves upon the pedestal of light and turns the other way.

   He faces towards the dark, and then the seven points of light within himself transmit the outward streaming light, and lo! the face of those upon the darkened way receives that light. For them the way is not so dark. Behind the warriors — twixt the light and dark — blazes the light of the Hierarchy. [31]

Linked with these sequential rhythmical festivals, each with its specialized inflow of specifically qualified spiritual and extraterrestrial energy, are linked the great universal and seasonal festivals recognized and celebrated by mankind throughout the centuries under various names. Outstanding examples are the midwinter and summer solstice festivals, which mark further 'in' and 'out' breaths of the type already referred to, and also the spring or Easter celebration and the experience of Pentecost, with their focus on resurrection and communication respectively. Of these last two, D.K. prognosticated:

The Festival of Easter and the Feast of Pentecost will be the two outstanding days of the religious year. Pentecost is, as you must well know, the symbol of right human relations in which all men and nations will understand each other — and though speaking in many and diverse languages — will know only one spiritual speech. [32]

Then there is the Wesak festival, usually held during May, according to the full-moon period at which it falls. In orthodox Buddhist circles, this is a memorial of Gautauma Buddha's life and work. In esoteric Buddhist and theosophical consideration, it is a living, perpetuated contact between the Father's House (the heavenly citadel of the Lord of the World of Tibetan esoteric tradition) and the Buddha as representative of the Will of God co-operating in ritual relationship with his brother, the Christ (the Maitreya Buddha) at the head of the hierarchical Lodge of Love. The Buddha and the Maitreya Buddha work together for the furtherance of the plan of unfolding love and enlightenment on earth. D.K. wrote of this:

The public should be educated in the knowledge of the relation of the Lord of Light and the Lord of Love to each other; the fact of illumination and the fact of loving understanding which these two outstanding Sons of God expressed should be emphasized; these divine qualities are the esoteric factors underlying goodwill. [33]

Occasionally, when it seems appropriate, a public tour or series of talks may be undertaken either by someone connected with the school or in relation to allied activities. One particular series undertaken by Foster Bailey in the late 1950s laid great emphasis on the *Changing Esoteric Values* (as the subsequent book was titled) that were motivating increased outgoing qualities and an accent on service to the human race as opposed to purely personal growth among students of the esoteric. However, this type of exercise is not considered as school classwork teaching but rather as a public outgrowth of it.

In the case of A.A.B.'s lecture work, the distinction appears less marked because her Secret Doctrine classes were one of the steps that led her towards the founding of her school and her fairly frequent speaking engagements were all part of the total effort to which her life was dedicated. We have already mentioned *The Consciousness of the Atom*, which is an example of an early series published in book form. Another series which received considerable acclaim were the talks she gave in New York on *The Twelve Labours of Hercules*, which dealt with the psychological significance of these tests in relation to the twelve signs of the zodiac.

While it is true that esoteric students generally find their way to a source of teaching by individual, self-forged paths — one here, one there, as the appropriate time gives them the opportunity — A.A.B. was occasionally presented with entire ready-made groups. Richard Prater, who was an associate of W.Q. Judge and an old pupil of Madame Blavatsky, caused his own Secret Doctrine class to join that of A.A.B. It was also he who passed her the papers in which she spotted Blavatsky's desire to put her esoteric teaching under the title 'Arcane School'. Another organization which linked itself with the school through seven senior members was India's Suddha Dharma Mandala, founded by Sir Subra Maniyer.[34] Although A.A.B. was, on her own admission, not a great joiner of organizations, she did apply to become a member of this one, which she felt was worthwhile. Having heard nothing from them, she later sent an order plus payment for some of their literature. This remained unacknowledged for three years, until suddenly, after she had given a public lecture in a Washington hotel, a man came up to her and delivered all the books she had ordered. No more was heard for some time until a letter came from a member saying that on his deathbed Sir Subra Maniyer, who had himself been studying A.A.B.'s *A Treatise on Cosmic Fire*, had instructed these particular members to put themselves under her tutelage.

By all accounts, and throughout her life, A.A.B. comes across as having been a natural performer in public. Apart from one or two sticky 'false starts' with the troops and some rather trying moments in her early evangelical days, she appears to have been able to hold her audience whether propounding the Bible, elucidating esoteric concepts or leading a singsong in an army canteen. In the final year of her life, she was still addressing full houses with dynamic authority. Even during the dark period in California, when she was without funds and entered a sardine canning factory in order to earn the money to keep her three small girls, she became so quick and nimble at the work that the management occasionally put her on show. (This she found was like being in a zoo, and sometimes her fingers trembled with anger at the slighting remarks made by visitors to the factory, remarks to which she was unable to answer back.)

One interesting interlude came in 1931 when Olga Fröbe-Kaptyn invited Alice and Foster Bailey to stay at her estate at Ascona on the shores of Lake Maggiore in Italy.[35] For three years a sort of summer school developed there and meetings were held in a specially built lecture hall. The contacts and exchanges that took place during this period helped considerably to extend the internationalization of the work. The group was quite small in the first year, but after that the activity got well under way and a number of influential people lent a hand, among them the promoter of psychosynthesis techniques in psychology Dr Roberto Assagioli, the popular British writer Violet Tweedale, authoress of *The Cosmic Christ* and the Russian Grand Duke Alexander, who wrote *The Religion of Love* (passages from which were used in Arcane School papers). All three were or became close friends of the Baileys. Later, Olga Fröbe-Kaptyn invited Jung, his colleagues and followers to make use of her facilities, and I believe a great deal of the material published in the famous Eranos yearbooks arose from work done in that location.

The summer of 1932 seems to have been a most significant period in relation to A.A.B.'s work, and she herself wrote:

In 1932 when we were at Ascona I received a communication from the Tibetan which was published in the fall in a pamphlet entitled *The New Group of World Servers*. This was epoch-making in its significance, though only a few people as yet realize its true meaning. [36]

This item postulated the existence of a group of world servers who are spiritually and subjectively united in purpose and intention without in any way being part of any super-organization or even necessarily known to each other on the outer levels of everyday existence. The concept appears in several places in A.A.B.'s writings. Those interested can find material under the subheadings 'The Law of Group Progress' in the second volume of *A Treatise on the Seven Rays* and 'Rule Ten' in *A Treatise on White Magic*, but the implications are so far-reaching and so closely interwoven with Alice Bailey's whole contribution that we will devote a chapter to the subject later.

However, the general concern prevailing within the school group in relation to the responsibility that all men and women of goodwill feel for human welfare and the way this was registered by those working around the Baileys after the close of world hostilities in 1945 brought the development of the school to a most interesting point. I remember seeing a copy of a letter sent out by A.A.B. about that time in which she called on students to invoke the forces of reconstruction and 'build, build, build' while picking up the threads and contacts of the work in a shattered world.

A.A.B. had by that time, with D.K., brought out an important book called *The Problems of Humanity*. This work sought to highlight the principles underlying the possible solution to a number of human problems of long standing: the psychological rehabilitation of nations, world reconstruction, racial minorities, relations between capital and labour, Church unity, the education of children, the opportunity of the United Nations and so on. While all these things are now the perpetual, non-fading headlines of our daily news bulletins, in the mid-1940s some of them were not allotted such universal consideration and made comparatively little impact on the minds of most people. A course of study was designed, based on this book, with the agreement of the group assisting at the school's headquarters office in New York. (By this time a penthouse suite on West 42nd Street, originally intended as a sports club and gymnasium, had been taken on. Initially, during the school's early period of growth, the space was shared with a Sufi order, so that A.A.B. and a spiritual friend, Hazarat Inayat Khan, had back-to-back shrine rooms.) The *Problems of Humanity* course was a pioneering and foresighted effort at that time. And within the context of the school work it was made absolutely obligatory to participate in this training. For a period of about two years, I believe, A.A.B. actually reduced the esoteric study, with the exception of the meditation work, in order that students should give full attention to these avenues of human need.

This in turn contributed to another significant event when on 21 September 1947 Djwhal Khul addressed himself in a fairly long letter to 'the students and workers of the Arcane School'. In the course of this letter he stated that, although he had played no part in the school's growth other than indirectly, through his writings via A.A.B., members of the Lodge had sought him out because it had attracted notice along three specific avenues:

a)   The response to messages written at the time of the Wesak festival year by year containing information on world service objectives.
b)   The distribution of material concerning the reappearance of the Christ, via the School. This subject was the basis of one of the books published through A.A.B.
c)   The decision to study the Problems of Humanity. This is, in

reality, a group effort to participate in the work of the Hierarchy and in its prime enterprise. The training of disciplines and the work in the Ashram is only incidental to *the work done for humanity.*'[37]

Perhaps it is not stretching imagination too far to see in these three a reflection of the triple thread of life, consciousness and creativity, or a resonant emblem of the interwoven objectives of meditation, study and service on which the school's whole effort and means for potential growth were rooted.

It is only proper to point out that, immediately after citing these examples, D.K. wrote:

As I point out to you these three encouraging events, I must at the same time point out that in them lies no cause for conceit, pride or self-satisfaction or for group congratulations; there is no opening in my words for the entrance of that unwholesome attitude of special privilege or of uniqueness which is the sad characteristic of many occult bodies. There is always present the sobering rememberance, is there not? that these events have come 'at long last', and might have taken place much earlier had the membership of the Arcane School and its workers, as well as of other esoteric schools and all spiritually minded people, been more 'heartily on fire' (using these words in their ancient and true import), and more alive and alert to human need. There is always likewise the recollection that the mass of human beings in the East and in the West *have* vaguely, nebulously yet truly (in their united millions down the ages) recognized the Wesak message of *the continuous presence on earth of the Hierarchy*, have cried their problems aloud to the spiritual men and women of the world with little avail, and have looked for the return of the Christ for two thousand years. All this has been present, though latent and oft deeply hidden; today, slowly the esoteric groups are awakening to the realization that their major service to humanity is to crystallize the immaterial, to render vocal and evocative the silent invocative recognitions of the masses of men and to stand, therefore, as a militant group between the attentive Hierarchy and expectant, suffering humanity.[38]

The echo of the ancient keynote used in relation to the meditative work at the time of the full moon comes through extremely loud and clear in these last few sentences.

Initially organized through one or two workers, various units of service sent out pamphlets, evoking a response where possible. Two channels of contact with the general public which Arcane

School students and others used to forward this general type of work came to be referred to as the service activities of the Arcane School. Having started to come into existence about ten years after the school's inception, in response to ideas presented in A.A.B.'s writings, these were gradually organized throughout the 1930s, kept going somehow or other during the world war and then reorganized more strongly along international lines after the 1940s.

These service activities are not obligatory to school students, but they are presented as available channels for constructive activity. The most tangible and down-to-earth was initially called 'Men of Goodwill' and is concerned with awakening the interest of intelligent men and women in human welfare, through the action of 'Units of Service' in many countries. These autonomous units of group activity are encouraged to highlight the principles on which thought-forms of solution could feed and develop. The work is therefore, in the broadest sense, educational. In the 1940s this large-scale effort had its own reading sets or papers on the nature of effective goodwill, prepared by one of A.A.B.'s daughters, Mildred Pugh. Later the name was changed to 'World Goodwill' and the work proceeded through the various centres in which the school established itself, in New York, London and Geneva. And today many units of service function wherever groups of individuals motivated by essential goodwill pick up the challenge of the work. Where these groups, which work on their own initiative and quite frequently in their own style based on the understanding of those who have taken responsibility, require any material, then World Goodwill, from the head-quarters office of the Lucis Trust — an organization created by Foster Bailey to be a legal entity for the burgeoning ramifications of the work — will supply some. The Trust does not run the units of service or answer for their actions, though it will offer guidelines and suggestions through World Goodwill if requested to do so. And various individuals who have taken responsibility for the World Goodwill work over the years keep up a steady stream of bulletins and brochures on particular subjects ranging through economic order, world hunger and other service items being handled by the United Nations. There are also occasional day seminars and workshops.

The other complementary, though more subjective, service activity is called Triangles. This will seem quite understandable to many nowadays because it is based on the increasingly familiar concept of networking, but this was not so much a part of general experience, even amongst people of goodwill, in 1938, when this phase of the work was getting under way. In simple terms, this is a pledge made amongst three people to link mentally at some point each day, even though their actual physical contact may be infrequent or nonexistent. Having linked up in imaginative contact, they use an invocation for light and love to illumine the human scene. This group of three offer a symbolic representation of the Trinity and is in fact the smallest 'group' that can exist (two being a polarity). Triangles is therefore a group activity, and it is also a networking one because each 'point' of a triangle can link with two others to form another triangle so that the practice spreads out to embrace the globe.

Originally, there was an idea of organizing triangles of light and triangles of goodwill, each representing subtly different energies. This, however, seemed overly complex and the whole activity then became known as a network of triangles of light and goodwill. The esoteric intention behind the service was that this invocative work carried forward in group formation would charge the vital-etheric atmosphere behind the dense physical appearance with the necessary vitality to support positively the more objective action of the goodwill units, and indeed that it should contribute in a deeper sense to the redevelopment of the etheric patterns of the world (from squares to triangles) in order to enhance energy flow. This is a subject that those interested can pursue elsewhere. [39] It is very much an activity carried forward in faith, with no immediate tangible result to spur the participant, and consequently a real test of working 'without attachment to the fruits of action'. Individual triangles can, of course, strengthen their linked relationship by simultaneously participating in other forms of service. And all members of the network can recognize that they are operating 'in love', which is a form of *'setsun'* or 'keeping good company'. D.K. mentioned at one time that this type of service could appeal with good effect [40] to the Japanese attitude of mind; however, while there have in the course of time undoubtedly been Japanese participating in the network, this service has not as yet taken fire from within that people.

All that we have discussed here implies rather a high level of dedication, which is why I have borrowed for this chapter heading a description of A.A.B. attributed to Christopher Isherwood by some Americans of his acquaintance. His own biographer[41] was unable to report any mention of Alice Bailey, although the Heard-Huxley Vedanta set were doubtless acquainted with theosophical teaching. A.A.B. would probably have described herself as a fellow student, and it must be clear that while her own upbringing was exceedingly strict and pure by contemporary standards, the whole emphasis on individual responsibility and impersonality could hardly have turned her into a governess. Moreover, while she certainly helped some good people, I doubt whether she produced many saints. In a metaphorical and a literal sense, where there is an increase of light (or enlightenment), an awareness of the fall of the shadow may also receive a sharpened emphasis, though this can be rectified as the 'sun' rises to its meridian. One of the school's practices involves a form of Pythagorean review which I have heard called 'the midnight tribunal'. The student is encouraged to unroll the day's experiences backward like a reversed film. He or she is not encouraged to moralize about what appears in the sense of applying condemnation or applause, but simply to observe quietly the connection between cause and effect.

Whatever dedication individual students may or may not bring to the school's work and aims, nothing outside their own considered intention is going to keep them in the school. This intention and the vision that sustains it are akin to the Boddhisattva vow referred to by Buddhists. The vow is of course a universal experience existing regardless of the trappings of any particular faith: from the depths of conscious being the vow is made to the spirit of life itself. If I may clarify this point with a quotation from another source, in order to give this matter some freshness through contrast, Chögyam Trungpa Rinpoche writes in *The Myth of Freedom*:

The stepping stone, the starting point in becoming awake, in joining the family of buddhas, is the taking of the bodhisattva vow. Traditionally, this vow is taken in the presence of a spiritual teacher and images of the buddhas and the scriptures in order to symbolize the presence of the lineage, the family of Buddha. One vows that from today until the attainment of enlightenment I devote my life to work with sentient beings and renounce my own attainment of enlightenment. Actually we cannot attain enlightenment until we give up the notion of 'me' personally attaining it. As long as the enlightenment drama has a central character, 'me', who has certain attributes, there is no hope of attaining enlightenment because it is nobody's project; it is an extraordinarily strenuous project but nobody is pushing it. Nobody is supervising it or appreciating its unfolding . . .

The bodhisattva vow acknowledges confusion and chaos — aggression, passion, frustration, frivolousness — as part of the path. The path is like a busy, broad highway, complete with roadblocks, accidents, construction work and police. It is quite terrifying. Nevertheless it is majestic, it is the great path. 'From today onward until the attainment of enlightenment I am willing to live with my chaos and confusion as well as that of all other sentient beings. I am willing to share our mutual confusion.' So no one is playing a one-upmanship game. The bodhisattva is a very humble pilgrim who works in the soil of samsara to dig out the jewel embedded in it. [42]

As we digest this point for ourselves we can return to a further remark made by D.K. in the course of his letter to the Arcane School:

As you study . . . I would have you bear in mind the long, long patience of the Christ and of His workers, the Masters, as they have awaited countless centuries for men to awaken to an intelligent analysis of the conditions which prevent the materializing of the Kingdom of God on Earth. [43]

In preparation work for the reappearance of Christ, the School offers, to those who may wish to use it, a meditation outline which contains the following dedication:

Forgetting the things which lie behind, I will strive towards my higher spiritual possibilities. I dedicate myself anew to the service of the Coming One and will do all I can to prepare men's minds and hearts for that event. I have no other life intention.

3. The Old Chestnut

In the same letter to the students of the Arcane School just quoted, Djwhal Khul added a fourth area of possible usefulness, and then took a further nine pages to amplify it. Having warmed to his subject, he clearly intended to make some impact. He approached the subject in this way:

It is perhaps a far harder task than that of studying world problems, spreading the knowledge of the Wesak Festival, and doing what can be done to prepare men's minds for the coming of the Christ. It is, however, something which must be undertaken prior to that coming because upon its success will depend the right and correct inauguration of the coming civilization. I do not say that this lies in the hands of the Arcane School membership; I am not so unintelligent or so sectarian in my attitudes. I *do* say that you can greatly help in a line of work which is engrossing the attention of the Master R. and of all the Masters upon the third ray. It is the task of regenerating Money. [1]

He then continued his discussion by tackling some of the objections so-called spiritually minded people have in relation to the subject of money and how to handle it in a balanced way. He pointed out as he did so that it was only a crystallized form of human energy and sometimes a purely symbolic representation for goods and services, his correction of the old adage 'Money is the root of all evil' being that it is not, any more than any other neutral force is of itself evil. [2] But he did say that 'the love of money' for its own sake can very well be so; in other words, it is simply our misplaced valuation that tips the scales in the wrong direction.

It was in discussing the mistaken belief that the spiritually minded should avoid the subject of money that A.A.B. used the term 'the old chestnut', which he did not know or really understand but recognized that people seemed to comprehend.

If we may slightly change the phraseology and rename money 'the hot chestnut', it could be called a subject of major interest. Whether we approach it in the guise of collective economics or of personal wealth, it is true that a huge number of individuals spend a majority of their waking hours trying to get the hot chestnut out of the fire; which, in terms of esoteric sensibility, means they are trying to learn the control of rough energy in a fairly crude material form, even though the techniques for handling that energy are often highly sophisticated. D.K. put it like this:

Money is the manifestation of energy. All energy can be applied in differing ways, being in itself an impersonal and blind force. It can be selfishly or unselfishly used. That, in itself, constitutes the main difference. Motive and creative thought determine the magnetic power of any individual, group or centre. [3]

If we recall that the hylozoistic concept implies that all is energy in different states, and that this appears to be a basis of the ageless wisdom stance, then perhaps we can accept that the use and misuse of energy is the way in which we build and destroy the environment around us. Money is one of the energies with which we can do this in a materially concrete way, and our responsibility in this respect to the world in which we exist is pivotal to A.A.B.'s outlook.

Throughout the written works, some of which we have quoted, Djwhal Khul would himself occasionally quote from other material to which he had access. Sometimes he would give the source, one of the most frequent being what he called *The Old Commentary*; at other times he would simply refer to 'ancient archives'. This last, so it would appear from the material given, covered a number of works. It is one such quotation which illustrates how an understanding of energy is a paramount factor in the development of consciousness; this quotation, judging by the altering syntax, would seem to be in translated form. Sometimes he spoke of references as being in Sanskrit or in an even older language which he called Sensa, [4] or sometimes, as with some of the formulas of revelation which we shall mention later, as being encapsulated in symbols. These he interpreted in English words and approximate diagrams, as best he could, through A.A.B. The curious, relevant passage about energy goes as follows:

Energy is all there is, O Chela in the Light, but is not known. It is the cause of knowledge and its application and its comprehension lead to expanded understanding.

Through energy the worlds were made, and through that energy they make progression; through energy the forms unfold and die; through energy the kingdoms manifest and disappear below the threshold of the world, which ever is and which will be forever.

Through energy the Cross is mounted and from the vortex of the four uniting forces, the initiate passes through the door and is propelled into the Light — a light which grows from cycle unto cycle, and is known as supernal Energy Itself. [5]

To some reading this book the philosophical implications of energy use may seem of more random and distant interest than how the Baileys handled their own cash flow. After all, despite the fact that the books dictated or influenced by D.K. may have had a limited public initially, as the years went by many thousands of copies went into circulation in several languages and the number of reprintings of certain volumes are already in double figures. This represents a remarkable achievement for any small publishing house, particularly for one handling esoteric subjects. A.A.B.-D.K. books were not all that the Lucis Publishing Company produced, even though Foster Bailey founded it primarily for the purpose of publishing, producing and selling the material D.K. entrusted to them: for example, an excellent dictionary of mythology was among their early titles. However, eventually the sheer quantity of what are sometimes referred to, rather loosely, as 'the Bailey books' left the fairly small work-force with little time for much else. How was this endless tide of publication sustained? The key factor was of great simplicity. A.A.B. never took any royalties. Her thirty years of co-operative work with Djwhal Khul was done, quite literally, for love. A financial pool called the Tibetan Book Fund was created, and any monies accruing after the payment of production costs went into the fund for future publications. Thus it was a revolving fund, breathing in and breathing out energy as the books were written, published, sold and reprinted. Of course, it was and is possible to contribute to this fund from outside the publishing circuit. When a new title was due or a fresh language edition had been prepared, friends of the work were able to give a boost to the proceeds by making a contribution towards the special project in hand. Nevertheless, the linchpin is the A.A.B.-D.K. co-operative effort and the self-sustaining basis of its foundation.

There have, naturally, been a number of people who acknowledged similar principles in founding enterprises and yet chose slightly different sustaining patterns in order to achieve their objectives. The Elmhirsts, who launched the Dartington Hall Trust with its many attendant projects, were particularly interested in raising the energy level within geographical districts; something Leonard Elmhirst had attempted to do in miniature while working for the Indian village project inspired by Tagore. Although Dorothy Elmhirst had money and spotted many brilliant people who were able to take charge of projects, I believe it was rare for them to continue pouring money into something that was not beginning to reach its objectives after a three-year period. And they tried as far as possible to balance each cultural project with a commercial one so that the two could march in step in a mutually supportive way.[6] The idea of profitable concerns adopting artistic/spiritual projects, as with the Carlsberg Lager Company and its cultural affiliates in Denmark, is becoming more widespread, but it is not yet as common a phenomenon as might be wished; in some countries, the idea of this sort of twinning would seem strange indeed.

The early efforts of what was originally a private co-operative allowing a full interplay between works and management (as was the case with the Scott-Bader company, I believe), resulted in a legal document that proved useful in setting up other unrelated trusts and companies. The establishment of any new pattern, albeit on an experimental basis, which has a fighting chance of successful operation creates a precedent. Each creative effort draws on what has gone before; it does not have to remain entirely within the range of experience of the one initiating the new undertaking. Each experimental effort helps its companion enterprises break new ground.

The Baileys' efforts in this respect were often based quite severely on sacrificial giving, but this was underpinned by A.A.B.'s own very real generosity. One of the objections I have heard from her friends concerning her attempts at autobiography is that she was simply unable to convey her own great quality of warmth, veiled as it was by personal shyness and a strong platform persona. A story is told of Madame Blavatsky being comfortably ensconced on the first-class deck of a ship bound for America when she became aware of a woman and child on the quay trying desperately to obtain passage. She rushed down, cashed in her ticket and went steerage class with the woman and her baby. Stories like this one, as much as those about her great righteous rages, contributed to her legend, A.A.B., being such a private person, shrank from any attempts at legend-building, yet the same outgoing, caring quality apparently possessed her. I have spoken with the eye-witness of one incident where, having been convinced of the necessity, she simply took from her neck a pearl necklace that had been given her and handed it over without another thought.

Service to others was, of course, a theme that was interwoven with A.A.B.'s strict Moor Park upbringing. She recorded from her childhood time there:

Several times a week when it was time to go for a walk, we had to go to the housekeeper's room for jellies and soup for some sick person on the property, for baby clothes for the new baby at one of the lodges, for books for someone who was confined to the house to read. This may be an instance of the paternalism and the feudalism of Great Britain but it had its good points. It may be a good thing that it has disappeared — personally I believe it is — but we could do with that trained sense of responsibility and of duty to others. [7]

Madame Blavatsky claimed along with D.K. that a growing sense of responsibility was one of the first indications of an awakening to the life of the soul. [8] The range of that particular sensibility may also be an indication of the extent to which the soul light is able to reach the world environment, in which we are all placed, in a practical way.

A similar guiding rule, based on 'free-will offering' seems to have been adopted in relation to Mrs Bailey's lecture work. This was at first entirely free of charge and followed a principle common to many spiritual institutions, not least Tibetan Buddhism, which states categorically that 'the teachings are priceless', therefore one cannot put a monetary value on them. (However, you may, within the conditions of our modern world, need to pay rent for the floor space on which to put your prayer mat.) Eventually the Baileys set an entrance charge of fifty cents on A.A.B.'s New York lectures, which at first cut the audiences by a half, successfully eliminating those who had simply dropped in to kill time. [9] The Arcane School and other groups modelled on it made and make no formal charge, and obviously in certain countries currency restrictions do not allow the circulation of funds. The papers are nonetheless sent to all those who sincerely wish to undertake the work and have the capacity for it. However, the needs of the work, in practical financial terms, are made known to all so that everyone may support it as and how they can.

Foster Bailey, I suspect, often infuriated well-meaning benefactors, who would set aside some block of shares they felt sure would accrue in value and bestow it on the school: the security would be sold at once and the cash energy released into the general flow. Just as amidst the trials of her early evangelical days, A.A.B. would continually ask herself 'what Jesus would have done'[10], so Foster Bailey could be said to have decided on the principle of 'laying all at the feet of the Lord' (though I do not recall him using that sort of terminology, except perhaps in a wry way). Considered quite apart from the pressure of immediate needs, this type of practice seems to reflect a particular step or stage on the path of human development. Joel Goldsmith, the Infinite Way teacher, often stated metaphorically that one could not live on 'yesterday's manna'.[11] Gurdjieff, I believe, in his learning period, allegedly adopted the rougher, tougher exercise of burning, at least symbolically, his remaining roubles at the end of the day's activity. There appear to be certain 'rules of the road' which are universal in application; nevertheless, while the principles behind them are inviolate in their own domain, they do not all apply all the time and in all places. Finding out which, where and how has a great deal to do with how we can handle our energy supply with wisdom.

Esoteric astrologers sometimes speak of a subject progressing round the zodiac on 'the reversed wheel'.[12] I take this to apply to those on 'the path' who have started to take their spiritual destiny in hand, are consciously constructing the antahkarana and are trying to co-operate with life's interior flow. What they do and how they handle the energy that becomes available to them is subject to a new degree of responsibility. Yet this is not just a matter of personal determination; it is as though, having entered a new area in the game of life, a new ritual stage in development commences to influence circumstance. I remember a very good man once telling me how he had made certain interior recognitions, decisions and subsequent dedications in his own life,[13] and having done so, many things in relation to outer life arrangements seemed to fall apart. Things did not work out at all clearly or neatly: at the very moment when he wanted to offer so much, he was blown hither and thither in a material sense.

In whatever shape or form it may appear, this influx of new energy (for that is what it really is, even though outwardly the reverse may seem to be the case) is a testing experience for anyone involved in it. Within one of the world's many spiritual organizations there is actually a stage within a practised ritual, sometimes called the trial of 'the broken —' whereby an impossible demand is made. In such circumstances of seeming impotence, as one may well imagine, the subject can soon become engulfed in miasmas of self-pity, hopelessness and other maladies of the psyche; but it is also possible to awaken new depths of compassion and empathy with others — which is one of the potentialities of suffering — and willingness to carry on somehow regardless of the outer circumstances. One could call the experience 'the making of bricks without straw'. [14] In discovering how to do this, within the energy of his own being, the pilgrim on the reversed wheel learns gradually how to be spiritually self-reliant so that he does not place his dependence on the normal props provided by outer circumstance. He accepts that the world does not owe him a living and sets about discovering what wealth there may be in his own nature and in developing creativity. The impact of the energy flow propelled by the interior effort can reshape outer circumstances.

Of course, the ways in which such experiences may manifest can vary infinitely according to each individual. A.A.B. began her first experience of married life as Mrs Evans, well supplied with clothes and jewellery; she thus stepped out of a background where personal material need was not a conscious problem. Like many people before her, she let go of all these possessions in order to care for her young family. [15] Difficulties of communication during the First World War further cut the links with family members who might have replenished supply, but her own self-reliance saw her through and took her to the sardine factory. Then, as she entered on the first steps of the enterprise that led to her world work, that experience passed and faded away and new contacts, new co-operative supporters and sources of funding for the work itself emerged. It was not by any means like switching from one radio programme to another, with everything solved overnight. At one time, long before the days of the 'friendly neighbourhood laundromat', the Baileys got up early each week to wash sheets and household linen. When A.A.B. had done well with a lecture, Foster would sometimes jokingly hand her five dollars pocket-money, and the rest went on the general expenses of their ministry: they were never Rolls-Royce gurus. The point at issue is really that of conscious attitude, and it is sometimes quite difficult for people to grasp what this attitude is all about, so different are the goals on which one's sights are thus focused from those that normal society conditions the individual into considering as important.

Looking at the trailblazing life experience of workers like A.A.B., one can get a rough idea of how life shapes these special junctions or turnings in the path. It is akin to — though, alas, not quite so simple as — Guy de Maupassant's splendid apocryphal story of the monk who, finding his monastery fallen on hard times, remembered an old country brew of his mother's and invented Benedictine. De Maupassant's tale has a secondary moral in that the monk regularly got drunk out of his mind sampling his concoction in the abbey cellars. The other monks, aware of the great practical benefits of his work for the Order, simply sang Mass in the chapel upstairs and pitched the volume of their devotions loud enough to drown out his drunken songs. Nonetheless, we cannot do it by proxy in the long run; eventually each one has for him- or herself to be both Mary and Martha. Even though there may be cycles when one of these lines of action predominates over the other, most of us seem to need to learn the songs of both the cellar and the chapel. And also, somehow or other — and no ready-made trick exists for handling the details — we have to get the two into rhythm.

As has been pointed out, the timing is not the same for everyone. Not all of us can say with St Paul: 'Having nothing, yet have I all things — through Christ.'[16] In time and space, universal supply is obviously not immediately available to all, whatever the potential may be. Life seems to have other lessons to teach which are better explained through the balanced handling of modest means, as well as through the harsher lessons of deprivation, until we ourselves have understood the forces generated by man himself that are the real deprivation. It is we who have to 'make an analysis of the conditions preventing the appearance of the Kingdom of God', as D.K. put it, preparatory to doing something about it.

Being a practical spiritual teacher, D.K. quite frequently wrote about financial problems. He included information in the personal letters he wrote via A.A.B. to certain students of his own. His work with these students was quite separate from Mrs Bailey's efforts with the Arcane School, and we shall mention it further in a succeeding chapter. For the moment, it will be of value to consider some of the suggestions made; They are, as one might expect, focused on the greater needs of world service rather than on individual cravings. In this respect, and having regard for the fact that so many men and women of goodwill are at different stages on the spiritual path, D.K. places considerable emphasis on group work in relation to money.

Some extracts from D.K.'s letters to one particular student who, it was suggested, could consider handling the financing of certain work which he proposed via A.A.B., are worth studying here. Although written in 1936, their relevance to several general factors touching us all, does not appear to have diminished:

This whole question of money is one of the greatest difficulty at this time and also one of the utmost simplicity. The difficulty is due to the wrong thought which, for generations, has been brought to bear upon the problem, leading to wrong attitudes, even among the most devoted disciples. The attitude of humanity to money has been coloured by greed, by grasping for the lower self, by jealousy, by material desire and by the heart-breaking need for it which — in its turn — is the result of these wrong attitudes. These wrong attitudes lead to the disastrous economic conditions which we find all around us. They are effects of causes which are initiated by man himself. In the re-generation of money and in the changing of man's attitude to it will eventually come world release. If this cannot take place, then some dire condition will arise; money (as we know it) will vanish off the earth and the situation will have to be met in some other way. Let us hope that this will not be needed but that it will be possible to change the thought of humanity where money is concerned so that it will be regarded as a great spiritual asset, as a definite spiritual responsibility and as a means to real world work. [17]

He then went on to try and sum up what he felt could be a helpful attitude for future action. Here he seems to have taken care to keep his discussion airborne above the tramlines of any particular school of thought, set of beliefs or techniques for acquiring money:

As money has in the past ministered to personal and family need, so in the future it must minister to group and world need. Each unit has, in the past, attempted to act as a magnet and to attract to itself that which will meet what it regards as its need — using personal activity and labour, if of no influence or education, and financial manipulation where that was possible. Groups in the future must act as magnets; they must see to it that they are animated by a spirit of love. I give you a thought here which is capable of much expansion. *Need, love and magnetic power are the three things which — consciously or unconsciously — attract money.* But they must all manifest at once. The need in the past has not always been real, though it has been *felt* (such is the world glamour and illusion). The love has been selfish or unreal; the demand for things material has been for that which is not necessary to health or happiness. The magnetic force utilized has been, therefore, wrongly motivated and this process — carried forward over so long a time — has led to the present dire financial situation in the world.

By the transmutation of these factors and the expression of their higher correspondence — through right love, right thought or meditation and right technique — the financial requirements of the new groups and of the New Group of World Servers *will* be found. [18]

Then D.K. expounded, as he had done in the letter to the Arcane School, about money as energy and of the need for understanding the magnetic value of motive and creative thought. Both of these, he continued, required appropriate preliminary meditation. And for this purpose, in order to aid clarification and because of the needs of the greater world work, he offered a reflective, meditative outline or guide. This has been taken up by Arcane School students and others who have read it in A.A.B.'s writings. It seems entirely appropriate to include it here:

Reflective Meditation on Attracting Money for Hierarchical Purposes

Stage I

After achieving a positive and intended personality quietness, formulate clearly to yourself and in your own words, the answers to the following questions:

1. If money is one of the most important things needed today for spiritual work, what is the factor which is at present deflecting it away from the work of the Hierarchy?
2. What is my personal attitude towards money? Do I regard it as a great and possible spiritual asset, or do I think of it in material terms?

3. What is my personal responsibility in regard to money which passes through my hands? Am I handling it as a disciple of the Masters should handle it? (*Pause.*)

Stage II

1. Ponder on the redemption of humanity through the right use of money. Visualize the money in the world today as
   a) Concretized energy, at present largely used for purely material purposes and for the satisfaction (where the individual is concerned) of purely personal desires.
   b) Visualize money as a great stream of flowing golden substance, passing out of the control of the Forces of Materialism into the control of the Forces of Light.

2. Then say the following invocative prayer, with focused mental concentration and from a *heartfelt* desire to meet spiritual demands:

   'O Thou in Whom we live and move and have our being, the Power that can make all things new, turn to spiritual purposes the money in the world; touch the hearts of men everywhere so that they may give to the work of the Hierarchy that which has hitherto been given to material satisfaction. The New Group of World Servers needs money in large quantities. I ask that the needed vast sums may be made available. May this potent energy of Thine be in the hands of the Forces of Light.'

3. Then visualize the work to be done by those groups which claim your present allegiance (i.e., the Arcane School and the Service Activities, or any other group which you know is attempting to carry out the hierarchical Plan). Then, through the creative imagination and by an act of the will, see untold and unlimited sums of money pouring into the hands of those who seek to do the Masters' work.

4. Then say aloud, with conviction and emphasis:

   'He for Whom the whole world waits has said that whatsoever shall be asked in His Name and with faith in the response will see it accomplished.'

   Remember at the same time that 'faith is *the substance* of things hoped for and *the evidence* of things not seen.' Then add:

   'I ask for the needed money, for . . . and can demand it because . . .'

   'From the Centre which we call the race of men Let the plan of Love and Light work out. And may it seal the door where evil dwells.'

5. Close with a careful consideration of your own responsibility to the Plan, and each week plan your financial co-operation with

the Hierarchy. Be practical and realistic and know that if you do not give, you may not ask, for you have no right to evoke that which you do not share.

Suggestions:

1. This meditation is so simple that many of you may regard it as innocuous and perhaps futile. Used by many simultaneously, it may shatter the impasse which at present prevents adequate funds pouring into the work which the Hierarchy seeks to accomplish.
2. Do this meditation every *Sunday* morning. Take what you have saved during the previous week and dedicate it to the work and present it in meditation to the Christ and His Hierarchy. Whether the sum is large or small, it can become an attractive and magnetic unit in the Masters' plans.
3. Realize the occult Law that 'to those who give shall be given' so that they can give again.
4. Attempt to feel true love sweeping through you, and have the fixed intention to express this love to all you contact. It is the great attractive and selfless agent in world affairs.[19]

In addition to this, he also offered a simple, searing invocation. In so far as any genuine *cri de coeur* can be put into words, this sought to channel the voiceless appeal of those touched by world need:

'Oh Thou in Whom we live and move and have out being, give of Thine abundance and let the work go on.' And with it goes a complimentary response: 'Oh Lord of Love and Light, touch our hearts anew, that we too, may love and give.'[20]

In this invocation, the innate image is on the divine circulatory flow, on Life itself, with supply simply an aspect of the abiding Tao of Life in which our existence finds its place. It is entirely impersonal; its effectiveness is dependent on a genuinely decentralized goodwill and an appreciation of the One work in which so many service groups have a contributory place. For some people, such phrases may very well be just another jumble of words and of little 'real' significance. However, I believe there are many working groups who accept, as we quoted earlier, that 'all that is, is ever present' and that furthermore we live in a universe which is a storehouse of all kinds of extraordinary energies. It is our attitude and our invention that are put to the test as we research and explore the place in which we find ourselves. Moreover, I believe that there is a fairly general recognition among many intelligent people of goodwill that no form of words, or of thoughts for that matter, is of itself going to provide a magic key to the storehouse. Nonetheless, such meditative formulas, prayers, or invocations, depending on how you look at them, can assist the expansion of consciousness, thus causing a shift in attitude which in turn influences action and the release of energy through the psyche. And through inspired action, new treasure can literally come to light.

Somewhere D.K. wrote with A.A.B. about the emphasis that ancient fraternities have often put on a future for the human race that could be graced by unity, peace and plenty. However, he stressed that it was in that order that these desirable attributes of life could be found; one could lead to the other in that order, but they rarely lasted without the proper sequential contribution being made by each one of them in strict progression. All such considerations have to be taken into account at the moment of invocation, together with the fact that the little personal self has to open itself as a clear, true channel.

Given clear motive and good intention in this last respect, two main techniques of giving and/or receiving were discussed by D.K.[21] One of these he termed the Way of the Buddha, illustrated by the begging bowl of the mendicant, which is of course to a fairly large extent the method used by a great number of our modern charitable organizations. The other he designated as the Way of the Christ, symbolized by the transformation of water into wine or change through creativity: that is, something definite is done in a work sense in order to bring money in. Each of these techniques has its place and value in financing service work.

Of course, every game in life can have its ace in a hole, its beneficient surprise or breakthrough during a crisis. Such happenings are not to be relied upon, though one of them is perhaps more likely to pop up at times of activity than in periods of inertia. I recall one occasion in the 1950s, some years after A.A.B.'s death, when many of the opportunities concerning the spread of the goodwill work foreseen by D.K. and herself were beginning to emerge and some aspects of the daily effort were stretched to penury. One morning an apologetic executive of the printers used by the Lucis Press came on the telephone to explain that a large number of unbound copies of *A Treatise on Cosmic Fire*, no less, had gone up in flames. A fire in some warehouse where the printer had stored them had turned them into a rather opportune burnt sacrifice. Fortunately they were not immediately required for sale, and there is no denying that the sudden appearance of a healthy insurance cheque in one of the company accounts could only create confidence in the bank handling allied accounts not currently so fortuitous. A gap in progress has often been bridged by an extraordinary leap in the dark; a spark can light the way.

On another, earlier, occasion, someone in America gave the Baileys the key to a deposit box and told them they might have the contents. This box had been lodged in the Chancery Lane Depository in London, which suffered badly from wartime bombing. The item in question had, however, been rescued from a corner ledge in a vault where it had lain for many years. Foster collected it and brought it back to A.A.B.'s room to open: it proved to be full of gold coins. They had to be declared as treasure trove, but nonetheless provided a very helpful fillip on the work front. Sometimes our own dormant energy can produce a treasure.

Whether we approach the subject of finance from the angle of the responsibility shown or not shown by individual men and women of goodwill and by service groups working here and there, or, as we shall now briefly try to do, from the angle of the world picture, the whole of A.A.B.'s writings illustrate a definite stance on the part of the Lodge. And on reading this material it becomes obvious that while the blessing of spiritual potential is always there, the course of events by which actual changes occur on the human scene is by no means an ongoing tale of sweetness and light. For instance, it has been made fairly obvious to the world at large that a clearly registered oil crisis can teach more lessons on ecological resources and the interrelation of international economies than can a great deal of sound advice. The latter is often available, but seldom listened to until crisis strikes; so it is best that we accept gratefully our continuing need for both the crook and the flail until we can successfully demonstrate that this is no longer the case.

In advancing into any slight consideration of the world economic position, we must, I think, for a moment remember our discussion of the science of impression as a means of human contact by the Lodge (see Chapter 1). World economics is the stuff of modern politics; at their most callous, both totalitarian and democratic methods of achieving power can turn into little more than a vulgar scramble for the money bags. Now, unless D.K.'s assurances of the Lodge's beneficient intentions are acceptable to us, any discussion of this aspect of A.A.B.'s message could, for some, raise spectres of 'Big Brother'-style manipulation: we are so entrenched in our divine right to do the clumsy thing in our own sweet way, are we not?

It is really difficult to write with any degree of reality about the goals and visions of conscious states quite different to our workaday world and yet at the same time register the concern which units of consciousness within such alleged realms may feel for those floundering in the mess we inhabit. Much that A.A.B. wrote down about what D.K. referred to as the externalization of the Hierarchy relates to future time. However, the material gives an indication of how the Lodge can sometimes operate in relation to human enterprise. The information given on one of the 'many mansions' is particularly interesting where the subject of finance is concerned, and a rough précis extract seems justified. The discussion concerns a Master who 'has always withheld his name from public knowledge'. The statement about this personage continues with a startling assertion about 'the Master who started what is called by you "the labour movement". This is regarded by the Hierarchy as one of the most successful attempts in all history to awaken the masses of men to general betterment, and thus set up a momentum which would, occultly speaking, 'swing them into light'. Later, in the same place, he goes on to say:

This Master works primarily with the intelligentsia, and he is therefore a third ray Master — upon the ray of Active Intelligence. His ashram is occupied with the problems of industry, and the goal of all the thinking, all the planning and all the work of impressing receptive minds is directed towards spiritualizing the concepts of the labour party in every country, and of industrialists, thus turning them towards the goal of right sharing, as a major step towards right human relations. This Master therefore co-operates with the Master R — who is the head of the third ray ashram, and who is also one of the triangle of forces which controls the greater ashram of the Hierarchy itself. The ashram of this Master (who has always withheld his name from public knowledge) is a lesser ashram within the major third ray ashram, just as my ashram lies within the ring-pass-not of the ashram of the Master K.H. [22]

D.K. also points out the natural involvement of this particular work with mass education, as a result of which, he maintains, the average modern citizen in the West is as well educated as was the intellectual of the Middle Ages. And at this point in his dissertation, he states:

You have, in this activity, an outstanding instance of how the Masters work, for (to the average onlooker) the labour movement arose from within the masses and the working classes; it was a spontaneous development, based upon the thinking and the teaching of a mere handful of men who were regarded primarily as agitators and trouble makers; they were in reality a group of disciples (many of them unconscious of their esoteric status) who were co-operating with the Law of Evolution and also with the hierarchical plan. They were not particularly advanced disciples, but they were *affiliated* with some ashram (according to their ray), and were therefore subject to impression. Had they been advanced disciples or initiates, their work would have been futile, for their presentation of the plan would not have been adapted to the level of the intelligence of the then totally uneducated masses composing labour. [23]

In another passage where he again refers to the work of the Master interested in the labour movement, he claims:

This work he began to do in the latter part of the nineteenth century, but left it to carry forward of its own momentum when Russia entered the field and laid an undue emphasis upon the proletariat during the revolution and in the later years of the first quarter of the twentieth century. [24]

The reason for this would seem fairly obvious: if guidance were tight and continuous, humankind would not be able to make the effort its own. It is our right to abuse the vision given, albeit to our own detriment. And this must, presumably, apply to the whole possibility of agents of the united Lodge functioning on the human scene. In an entirely human way, they would need to be invoked into manifestation, not as genii from Aladdin's lamp but as spirit working within the human race. This is not a matter of conjuration; just the truth behind the tired old cliché that we tend to get much of the leadership we collectively tune in to. In some concluding remarks about this subject and its relation to the loosely knit international labour movement, D.K. wrote:

It is well to bear in mind that all great movements on earth demonstrate both good and evil; the evil has to be subdued and dissipated, or relegated to its right proportional place, before that which is good and in line with hierarchical planning can find true expression. What is true of the individual is true also of groups. Before the soul can express itself through the medium of the personality, that personality has to be subdued, controlled, purified and dedicated to service. It is this controlling, subduing process which is going on now, and it is vociferously fought by the selfish and ambitious elements. [25]

D.K. listed three key themes which would need to qualify any successful co-operation with this overall effort, namely right motive, selfless service and intelligence. He mentioned also the contribution that this ashram of spiritual workers make in dissipating and offsetting evil at the human level, in 'sealing the door where evil dwells' (as the stanza of an invocation promoted by A.A.B. puts it, in the course of the reflective meditation previously quoted), saying:

It is essentially this group which (if I dare so express it) is coping with raw materialism and the false values which it engenders. The door has to be sealed by a vast mass of co-ordinated human forces, and not by one or two enlightened men. This fact must be grasped by you . . .

The group is occupied with worldwide economic problems, and also with a direct attack upon the basic materialism to be found in the modern world. The problems of barter and exchange, the significance of money, the value of gold (a basic symbol of the third ray of active intelligence), the production of right attitudes towards material living, and the entire process of right distribution are among the many problems dealt with in this ashram. [26]

A main weapon — and I think the use of this word is a just one — employed by the opposing force within mankind that militates against the new incoming energetic potential is analysed by D.K. in his attempt to give the point of view of his fraternal co-workers along this lineage. He claims that it:

is chaos, disruption, lack of established security, and consequent fear. The potency of these evil forces is exceedingly great because they belong to no one group of people and to all the ideologies. The chaos produced by indifference, the chaos produced by uncertainty, the chaos produced by fear, by starvation, by insecurity, by watching others suffer innocently, and the chaos produced by the warring and conflicting ambitious elements in every nation *(without exception)* — these are the factors with which the Master R. is attempting to deal; the task is one of supreme difficulty. The entire rhythm of international thinking has to be altered, and that constitutes a slow and arduous task.[27]

In this respect words written in the 1920s have a particular relevance to our present time and to those who choose, for whatever reason, to throw in their lot with forces employing terrorist disruption to achieve their objectives. D.K. wrote of 'the reaction which will be set up . . . against crime, sovietism, and the extreme radicalism which is now being made use of by certain powers to achieve ends contrary to the plans of the Lord.'[28]

We have perhaps quoted enough from source to make this particular point. It is only one factor in the mass of material which A.A.B. was responsible for producing, and is connected with the work of the particular household lineage in which she had her own spiritual home, simply in so far as all ashrams help each other and effect change in human consciousness. Yet these matters have an intensely practical aspect and should be within everyone's grasp. (I am aware, nonetheless, that it would not be appropriate to overload this book with one set of the many signposts D.K. set up: people can get bored. There was an alleged incident when Ernest Bevin, who became the UK's post-war foreign minister, reportedly felt it necessary to tell George Lansbury, a founding figure of the British Labour movement, not to parade his soul at party conference.) And, indeed, D.K. gives hints about several of the other households to be found within the overall Lodge Mansion. Those reading these indications of the effort which he maintained was going on persistently behind the scenes are bound, regardless of whether they approve of these ideas or not, to seek in it something of personal relevance as well as of a more general interest. The query may well be raised that if, even for the sake of hypothesis, there is the merest ghost of a chance of D.K.'s account of things actually being true, what on earth can the individual do about it?

A sensed affiliation with any line of service or a response to a recognized need can draw one into the orbit of a particular spiritual effort. An entire one-hundred-page section of one of A.A.B.'s books, dealt with stages in the approach of a disciple to the work centre or ashram with which connection had been made and with relationship to 'the head of the household'. As this is a rather esoteric subject and we have transposed enough for one chapter, it may be best just to give the poetic phrases which designate each stage and leave the reader to conduct some enquiry with the right hemisphere of the brain, should there be the inclination: 'Little Chelaship', 'Chela in the Light', 'Accepted Chela', 'Chela on the Thread', 'Chela within the Aura' and 'Chela within the Master's heart'. A.A.B. also informs us: There is a later stage of still closer identification, where there is a complete blending of the Lights, but there is no adequate paraphrase of the terms used to convey this name. [29]

The subject is also dealt with in the writings of Helena Roerich, who recorded the Agni Yoga series of teaching books. [30] One point she made indicated that before a disciple was accepted by the teacher, he or she must be an 'accepting disciple'. Perhaps this gives the vital clue and also shows that there is nothing weird, no mysterious secret ceremony, but that it is all basically very simple: anyone wishing to help good work grow simply joins in. In the place where you are, and with the resources at your disposal, you make a start. Not exactly self-appointed, the development is more a case of being soul-induced. One of A.A.B.'s associates, Regina Keller, was keen on suggesting that students take some cherished assumption and look at it reversed or at least put a query mark at the end of it. In reflecting on the phrases just given, why not try this practice? Taking the last heading first, turn it around and put a query at the end; you can then ask: 'Who is 'the Master in the Chela's heart'? If one remembers the Masters as shepherds of the life force and looks to the kind of service or the work-lineage to be energized, this in no way contradicts the material quoted in Chapter 1. [31]

In Tibetan interpretations of Vajrayana Buddhism, the visualization of particular deities and enlightened ones in relation to the psychic centres of energy within each being that require liberation is a practice adopted in invoking the beneficent qualities of the Buddhas. [32] Right at the start of the Arcane School work there is a simple meditation on the Master in the heart. The emphasis is on the immanence of divinity, as we have pointed out; however, there are many levels of identification at which this ancient practice can be approached. Thus an idea that is central to the whole body of teaching, with many levels of implication, comes right at the beginning of the work. The ensuing stages of growth are worth investigating. [33]

There will of course often be mistakes, faults in research, blind alleys, false images and illusory tasks which seem important at the time, but the work goes on; clarity can grow with effort and with the rough handling each of us receives from experience. This is particularly true when it comes to handling funds. Let us suppose, for the sake of discussion, that someone is convinced a task is worthwhile and is a suitable avenue for making a contribution to the common weal; and that moreover they see a chance of making it work practically within the context of the environment with which they are familiar. Getting it all together, which includes assembling whatever financial energy may be required for successful operations, is the precise lesson that the potential creative worker has to confront. In this way the work is learnt in the doing of it, without the door being in any way shut on the beneficent grace of spirit, in whatever form and at whatever time this may manifest.

Earlier we quoted a letter from D.K. via A.A.B. to a disciple in which he discussed the approach to finance dealt with in this chapter. In an earlier letter to the same person, three phrases or seed-thoughts for meditative reflection were offered as work aids:

1. Transfigure life in terms of accomplishment. True accomplishment involves a life of steady radiance.
2. There must ever be crises of achievement which will draw upon the full resources of the soul. These must be demanded by the personality.
3. Understand the technique of an aligned personality, for the extremity of the disciple in service draws out finally the interest of the soul. [34]

Now let us review what has been discussed here and break it all down into penny numbers, as it were. Just as with the building of the antahkarana, so with the question of financial supply (which can relate particularly to the creative aspect of that inner instrument), there are certain roughly defined phases:

a) There is dedication to the inward vision. There may at this time be a sense of lack and limitation, a seeming falling away of resource. And while the begging bowl may be required to get one through one's round of tasks, the lesson is one of soul-reliance and learning the ability to carry on despite the chaos of outer circumstance.

b) The stabilizing of the inward understanding, which allows one to 'see-through' any hold-up or blockage to the work until co-operative creativity and achievement again aligns the worker with nature's plenty. This is something of an act of faith that providence's abundance can be found on the other side of self-seeking.

Other stages in the alignment with energy lie ahead, but these factors seem to give a rough rule of thumb for the immediate steps ahead.

c) Each individual, on his own initiative, puts themselves through these paces. They dive into the work, as it were, to fill a gap with their own substance. D.K.'s thesis would seem to be that the general attitude to wealth and resource, as well as the energy of substance itself, is thus transformed and transfigured.

Yet it is at this point that we can spot a major gap to be bridged, one that relates as much to time as to economics. We may agree that a) and b) above are more or less accurate reflections of some people's experience. The question must nonetheless arise: will the needed shift in general attitudes take place in time for the health and well-being of the human family and the planet on which we live, move and have our being?

It could be said, if we again refer to what A.A.B. has recorded, that this question remains an open one within the Lodge itself. Returning to the document with which we started this chapter, [1] we note that D.K. concluded his discussion of the various projects that had been of interest to the Lodge and with which he claimed students could become co-operatively involved — the regeneration of money in the world was one — as follows:

The emphasis of the teaching lately going out from the Hierarchy to Humanity has ever been *world service* and the furthering of the attempt to prepare mankind for the coming civilization and for a sane and useful recovery from the horror of the past two centuries. To you, the horror probably consists in the massacre and agony of the past two wars or rather of the one great world war (1914-45). This war has disturbed the twentieth century and set it apart as the outstanding example not only of the working of the law of cause and effect but also of the poor judgment and the lack of understanding which characterizes modern man. Nevertheless, to us who have looked on at world affairs for so long a period, the true horror was the static state of human effort and living which preceded the mechanical revolution during the middle of the Victorian era. That frightful condition we made every effort to break; the emergence of modern world business through the manufacture of the machine was one of our efforts; the galaxy of poets, musicians, painters and writers which appeared at that time was another attempt on our part to disclose the hideous ugliness in the midst of which these expressions of beauty had to work. The machine which should have been an instrument of release became an engine of slavery; the beauty which should have dispelled the ugliness failed to do so.

Men marched forward on their selfish, ugly, aggressive way, turning everything contacted or discovered into fresh instruments whereby to satisfy their material inclinations and feed the underlying greed. They thus precipitated the two world wars and *set in motion a great cleansing agent*. It remains to be proved, however, whether the needed cleansing and the re-orientation of motives has been effective. We are hopeful that it has and are proceeding on that basis. [35]

A Mantram of Unification

The sons of men are one and I am one with them.
I seek to love, not hate;
I seek to serve and not exact due service;
I seek to heal, not hurt.

Let pain bring due reward of light and love.
Let the soul control the outer form and life and all events,
And bring to light the love which underlies the happenings of the time.

Let vision come and insight.
Let the future stand revealed.
Let inner union demonstrate and outer cleavages be gone.
Let love prevail.
Let all men love. [36]

4. Discipleship in a New Age

The fact of war and the 'four grim horsemen' who ride in its wake is a particularly hard subject for many spiritually inclined people to stomach. The attitude implicit in the passage quoted at the end of the last chapter cannot be taken to imply a callous attitude adopted from a detached Olympian position. When warfare broke out in 1939 and A.A.B. sent out pamphlets containing material received from D.K. which was not acceptable to pacifist friends, she was accused of doctoring it to suit pro-British attitudes. (In the dark days of European invasion D.K. had referred to the gathering of allies 'in that small fortress of the Forces of Light which is the British Isles'.[1]) She denied this charge[2] vigorously, however. In answer to those critics who said that God being love He must love all equally, she later wrote:

Because God is love, He had no alternative, or the Hierarchy either, working under the Christ, to do anything but stand firmly on the side of those who were seeking to free humanity from slavery, evil, aggression and corruption. The words of the Christ have never been more true, 'He that is not with me is against me'.

She pointed out that the cruel atrocities and enslavement policies revealed at the end of the war entirely vindicated D.K.'s stand.

When D.K. wrote that 'death is not the worst fate that can befall a human being,[3] he was certainly not playing the Victorian moralist. Elsewhere, in relation to the healing of sickness,[4] he added that we have to recognize that sometimes death is the cure. On the whole, though, his attitude towards death was a conventional one — conventional, that is, to the mainstream of ageless wisdom teaching, not to the rather muddled thinking of contemporary society:

Death, if we could but realize it, is one of our most practised activities. We have died many times and shall die again and again. Death is essentially a matter of consciousness. We are conscious one moment on the physical plane, and a moment later we have withdrawn onto another plane and are actively conscious there. Just as long as our consciousness is identified with the form aspect, death will hold for us its ancient terror. Just as soon as we know ourselves to be souls, and find that we are capable of focusing our consciousness or sense of awareness in any form or on any plane at will, or in any direction within the form of God, we shall no longer know death. [5]

In the above we have an echo of the traditional stand of the spiritual classic *The Bhagavad Gita*, wherein the warrior Arjuna is addressed upon the battlefield by Krishna:

Your words are wise, but your sorrow is for nothing. The truly wise mourn neither for the living nor for the dead.

There was never a time when I did not exist, nor you, nor any of these princes of men. Nor is there any future in which we shall cease to be.

As has been pointed out (unfortunately I cannot recall by whom, so I am unable to acknowledge their wisdom) life and death are not opposites: birth and death are polar events and both are incidents in the course of life.

D.K. discussed the subject of death and dying in a number of places throughout A.A.B.'s books, [6] and for the fourth volume of *A Treatise on the Seven Rays* a compilation of some of the main points was put together at his suggestion. Though it is a considerable issue of some practical moment to us all, we will not dwell on it at length here. Yet it is of some interest that the very difficult task of nursing those with extended terminal illnesses, made more pronounced by the ability of modern medical science to prolong life in the physical body, is causing the Western world to re-examine its attitudes to the process of dying. Pre- and post-natal care rightly get a great deal of attention, but the other end of our span is still something of an absent-minded and haphazard despatch. The Venerable Sogyal Rinpoche, one of the several religious teachers brought up in the Tibetan Buddhist tradition and now working in the West, received some training in the oral instruction and the rituals for assisting transference of consciousness at the moment of death which are intended to accompany the study of the Bardo, the *Tibetan Book of the Dead.* He is,[7] I know, keen to see this ancient knowledge integrated and evaluated in relation to modern science, as well as with the studies being pursued through the hospice movement and through the experience of such people as Dr Elisabeth Kubler-Ross, who have placed a special focus on the subject.

D.K. indicated[8] that the ancient art of dying (safeguarded in Tibetan lore) would come into its own with the growth of more enlightened attitudes to death, and he wrote: 'It is my hope that students will do something of major importance to aid in bringing forth the light upon the processes of death which humanity is today demanding.'[9]

He also wrote, touchingly, to students of his own:

I would ask you as life proceeds and you face eventually and inevitably the discarding of the vehicle, to hold increasingly on to your knowledge of the Hierarchy and thus pass over to the other side with complete dedication to the hierarchical plan. This is not simply suggestion on my part; it is an attempt on my part to call to your attention the concept of a spiritual continuity of knowledge and of a rightly oriented attitude.[10]

Another integral ageless wisdom concept which is evoked by the subject of death, as well as by the passage at the end of the last chapter, is the subject of karma and rebirth. An acceptance of the fact of reincarnation and the continuity of existence is sprinkled like aromatic herb throughout the A.A.B. writings. Sometimes, it will receive a special mention, as for example in *The Reappearance of the Christ* where it is highlighted as one of the subjects the coming Maitreya Buddha will elucidate for the world's population.[11] The matter-of-fact mention, given in the last chapter, of the law of cause and effect in relation to the world war is the sort of statement we find again and again, where the subject is taken for granted. However, this law does receive a great deal of explanation, including some very abstruse commentaries on the subject of karma, in *A Treatise on Cosmic Fire*.

In this respect, the four horsemen of the Apocalypse are simply the dark aspect of what D.K. calls the four Lords of Karma whom he attempts to rename[12] in a modern allegorical way as Enlightenment, Relationship, Pain and Return. For our present

purposes those unfamiliar with the concept of karma or the idea
of cause and effect working throughout life and beyond death
will perhaps find Charles Kingsley's creations Mrs Do-as-you-
would-be-done-by and her harsher sister, who took over
instruction when a lesson remained unlearnt, Mrs Be-done-by-
as-you-did, make the point without undue complication. [13] There
is also an old theosophical adage that 'If you look after the dharma
(the soul's task or spiritual job), the karma will look after itself'
because, as D.K. puts it, 'Love brings all earthly karma to an
end'. [14] M.J. Eastcott and Nancy Magor, who have been greatly
influenced by A.A.B.'s teachings, have as a support to their other
activities produced a number of small booklets. Among these
are *The Phenomena of Death* and *Pain and its Transforming
Power*, which examine these subjects in a fairly straightforward
and clear-sighted way. [15]

The subject of death is nevertheless only one instance of the
way in which the whole of D.K.'s teaching is governed by the
perspective he holds out for man. Clearly his programme of work
and A.A.B.'s co-operating effort together with the ground swell
of interest she created are buoyed up, by what for them is a
magnificent horizon. The whole immense, detailed operation
comprising the many books and the activities that sprang from
their varied concepts seems to be an attempt to share this vision
of life's potential and to explain ways in which it can be realized
as a factor of real, tangible use in man's daily business. D.K.
himself patently understood the paramount need of putting this
point across. Yet although his analysis of the problem is quite
easy to accept, his statements on the aims in view are so
overwhelming and literally so far-reaching that students can
hardly be blamed for retreating in to the safety of whichever items
of detailed teaching are for them a familiar haven. This is another
reason why individual accounts of 'Alice Bailey's teaching' are
so infinitely varied. Readers can judge this for themselves from
the following:

One may ask (and rightly ask) wherein all this information can be of
use to us in the midst of a troubled and bewildered world. For obvious
reasons, a vision of the divine plan, nebulous as it must necessarily be,
confers a sense of proportion and also of stability. It leads to a much-
needed re-adjustment of values, indicating as it does, that there is
purpose and objective behind all the difficult happenings of daily life.

It broadens and widens and expands the consciousness, as we study the great volume of the planetary life, embracing as it does the detail and the finished structure, the item man, and the entire life of the planet, with their relation to the greater whole. This is of far more importance than the minute detail of the human being's individual capacity to grasp his own immediate place within the larger picture . . .
The objectives can (for our purposes) be stated as four in number, but each of these is capable of re-expression in a number of ways . . .

1. The first aim and the primary aim is to establish, through the medium of humanity, an outpost of the consciousness of God in the solar system . . .
2. To found upon earth (as has already been indicated) a powerhouse of such potency and a focal point of such energy that humanity — as a whole — can be a factor in the solar system, bringing about changes and events of a unique nature in the planetary life and lives (and therefore in the system itself) and inducing an inter-stellar activity.
3. To develop a station of light, through the medium of the human kingdom in nature, which will serve not only the planet, and not only our particular solar system, but the seven systems of which ours is one . . .
4. To set up a magnetic centre in the universe, in which the human kingdom and the kingdom of souls will, united or at-oned, be the point of most intense power, and which will serve the developed great lives within the radius of the radiance of the One about whom naught can be said.[16]

You can see what I mean; while such statements may very well offer readers general unlift and a proper sense of horizon, they are also something of a put-down. If true on any terms at all, they indicate the primitive state of man's development, the adolescent quality of his greatest civilizations and the distance he still has to travel to come near target range — it is no wonder that individual students grab for particulars, in the way that a man on the rapids seizes a log in order just to keep afloat. People want to find out where they fit in; they would sometimes like to find 'their' work in the flow, even though any sense of proprietary right inevitably causes the log to slip from one's grasp. It is nonetheless understandable that they should wish to learn how to identify with the mainstream of human destiny. They may very well feel inspired and want to make this vast enterprise in some way their own. The way to do this would seem to be initially through what D.K. called 'expansion of consciousness', what we might call attempting to embrace the bigger picture and the longer view or, as we have already seen, the growth of the antahkarana. The more stupendous the horizon to be embraced, the greater must be the growth in consciousness in order to take it in. The more magnificent and far-reaching the enterprise, the more the individual has to relate and synthesize within his own awareness: a vast yet subtle dendrite bridge-building is required. It is with these relationships in consciousness that D.K.'s teaching contribution seems to be concerned in principle. And he admitted that his group of co-workers had been tagged 'the ashram of right human relations'.[17]

In fact, a very full record of D.K.'s approach to individual tuition and guidance exists in two volumes, both close to eight hundred pages long.[18] Despite the fact that he took no part in the organization of the Arcane School and had only an indirect and impersonal influence on its affairs through his teachings and a single letter, he did have a group of students of his own. For these particular individuals A.A.B. acted as a sort of secretary, distributing material of a general nature as well as a number of individual letters. In her foreword to the first volume of *Discipleship in the New Age* she made a personal statement about this group:

Many of these people were unknown to me when they were brought to my notice; some of them I have since met; others I have never met; some I knew well and could understand why they had been chosen, knowing that their dedication to the life of the spirit and their love of humanity warranted the choice; one or two were regarded by me as most unsuitable choices but later I altered my point of view and recognized that a wiser mind than mine was responsible for their inclusion in the ashram. I learnt also that ancient relationships, established in other lives, were also conditioning factors and that some had earned the right to inclusion, even if their spiritual attainments seemed inadequate to the onlooker.[19]

D.K.'s own exact, and exacting, remarks on the matter are of considerable interest, particularly as so much of what is in this book seems to concern A.A.B.'s connection with the Lodge:

The devotion of a disciple to some particular Master is of no importance to that Master or to his ashramic group. It is not devotion or predilection or any personality choice which governs the formation of a Master's group. It is ancient relationships, the ability to demonstrate certain aspects of life to demanding humanity and a definite ray expression of quality which determines the hierarchical placement of aspirants in an ashram. [20]

At the end of batches of letters again in the first volume, a brief note gives readers some idea of what has become of the individual concerned. The backgrounds of these people were obviously quite varied, and the directions from which they came in a religious respect were not the same, some assisting with the Arcane School whilst others clearly had projects and concerns of their own, established before their contact with A.A.B. The initials given before each set of letters are not the true ones and some dates are stated to have been altered. [21] These people have, to some extent, literally bared their souls in allowing the publication of this correspondence; and confidentiality concerning their identity has been strictly preserved. In a certain sense, the letters and other communications published in the two volumes of *Discipleship in the New Age* are ashram papers, though they do not represent a full record of the life and consciousness of an ashram. D.K. certainly had other work and groups, not to mention the duties of his workaday life. He wrote: 'I would remind you also that there are many members of my ashram of whom you know nothing and who came into my ashram without the help of A.A.B. You are not the group of major importance. Forget not these co-disciples.' [22]

D.K. pointed out that at the time of writing the ashramic work of right human relations had attracted five other Masters of similar status to his own and that he acted simply as the 'governor', the *nautonier*, or in his own phrase, 'the custodian of the plan'. [23]

If at certain points in this research I tend to quote overmuch, the reader must forgive the practice; we are dealing with what is obviously an abstruse and, especially where technicalities are concerned, extremely subtle consideration. There is absolutely no satisfactory alternative but for each one of us to wrestle with the presented ideas for himself if we are to stand a fighting chance of dealing with the work A.A.B. anchored, in the hope of sparking fresh developments within innate human potentiality. D.K. did not design his teaching to be conveniently packaged in pre-digested bite-size morsels.

In the same series of letters which we are now discussing, D.K.

took a great deal of trouble to make clear the essential difference between an ordinary human group enterprise and a true ashramic relationship, by emphasizing a factor which causes ashramic integration:

Unanimity of purpose produces a very close subjective relationship, and each member of the ashram is occupied with making his fullest possible contribution to the task in hand. Personalities do not enter in. You will remember how some years ago I told you that the personality vehicles are ever left outside the ashram — speaking symbolically. This means that the subtler bodies of the personality have perforce to follow the same rules as the physical body — they are left outside. Remember also that the ashrams exist upon the plane of buddhi or of the intuition. The joint undertaking and the united adhering to the desired and arranged cyclic technique binds all members of the ashram into one synthetic whole; there is therefore no possible controversy or any emphasis upon individual ideas, because no personality vibratory quality can penetrate in the periphery or the aura of an ashram. [24]

A seed-thought offered for meditation really sums up this point in a way which, while it is conducive of interpretation at many levels (as is the way with seed-thoughts), is yet comprehensible to everyone: 'The way of outer service is the way into the inner sanctum.' [25] For this reason I am choosing to discuss D.K.'s own group experiment almost entirely in terms of the projected programme of group service work. This is reasonably practical, factual and safe, and eventually a sure path through for those who may care to follow the trail.

Publication of the *Discipleship* books was decided on in order to demonstrate how the work proceeded and the principles on which it was based, and also to illustrate through case histories the development of individuals along the lines of the ray energies which influenced their equipment. [26] Moreover the whole effort, being a somewhat unique pathfinding experiment, is of decided value to those coming afterwards. Landmarks are identified and blueprints for future enterprise are on display, making it of definite interest to today's reader. Certain important matters nevertheless await our research. This is indicated in the rather terse note delivered by D.K. towards the close of A.A.B.'s cycle of availability (it is listed as having been written in March 1949, approximately eight months before A.A.B. passed on). The work had obviously been tough, and in his own way he challenged his workers to get on with their incomplete assignments:

I have no group instructions for you now. Nor shall I have again. When the instructions on the designated themes are completed, I will write an instruction upon group work which will close all that I have to say on the subject in the two volumes of the book *"Discipleship in the New Age"*. The major intention of this book is to awaken the aspirational public to the opportunity for training which is theirs *if* they so choose; it should make them think with greater clarity of the Hierarchy and its functions; much good may come of sending forth its teachings and a new era in the field of spiritual instructions may result. My present objective is now to help A.A.B. conclude the important teaching which I have — with her aid — been giving to the group over a long period of years; it will then be available to the general public, after certain specific deletions about which she knows and which are similar to those in the first volume. You have had more, much more, than you can assimilate; of the original group of students only a few are left; of the more than fifty original members who have been affiliated with my ashram, only sixteen remain, and of these only eight are truly active. [27]

Some people have told me that they feel saddened by this, particularly in view of the extraordinary chance this group seemed to have had to play a part in the evolutionary experiment D.K. called the externalization of the ashrams, briefly referred to earlier. But who can suppose that they might have been the ones to do better had the opportunity been found along their path? Quite aside from the exigencies of daily life and the difficulties of a world in conflict, the inward pressures in this sort of experiment would be considerable. In any event, it is all water under the bridge, literally and metaphorically, and we can take it, I believe, that the challenge implicit in the above statement is intended for those of the interested and intelligent public whose day of opportunity is now.

The very first section of the first volume has the general heading 'Talks to Disciples' and contains a sketch of D.K.'s whole approach to the experiment he was initiating. In the course of this he emphasizes many of the principles and proven methods through which group work is likely to be successful. He then went straight on to outline a plan for certain seed-groups. Rather in the way that a seed-thought exists at a more abstract level, a seed-group, as its name implies, is a pilot project. It is an act of faith, for, like Christ's analogy of the grain of mustard seed, it has unfathomed potential. Elsewhere[28] D.K. actually called them 'pattern-groups'. I have chosen to pick up this work on the plan for the groups because the subject of groups is obviously fundamental in a book that has been requested to examine visions of human potential, as this one has. We had better begin by examining the original statement:

I have said that these groups constitute an experiment. This experiment is fourfold in nature and a concise statement about it may prove helpful.

1. They are an experiment in *founding or starting focal points of energy* in the human family through which certain energies can flow into the entire race of men.

2. They are an experiment in *inaugurating certain new techniques in work* and in *modes of communication* . . . [There then follows several pages listing the groups and their possible function; we will return to this.]

3. These groups are also *an externalization of an inner existing condition* . . . [This point also receives some elaboration, and we will deal with it before the groups themselves.]

4. These groups are also an experiment which has for its objective the *manifestation of certain types of energy* which will, when effectively functioning, produce cohesion or at-one-ment upon earth.[29]

Much of the material D.K. expanded upon seems to have been laid down well before his own students were in a position to make use of it. His eye was on the whole range of the experiment as well as, one can only suppose, on the possibilities for future work.

He was evidently not alone in his application to the potential of these groups, for others besides himself envisioned their usefulness.[30] It may be worth while to give one of the detailed listings offered by him under the heading of item 3 above. While groups of men and women of goodwill active now are in no position to revive D.K.'s own experiment, even if they wanted to, the opportunity to apply to the same source motivation which he drew on surely remains open; as the nursery saying has it: 'A cat can look at a king.'

I wonder, my brothers, if the following sequence of statements will convey anything to your minds? It is a statement of fact and is not the least symbolic in its terminology — except in so far as all words are inadequate symbols of inner truth.

1. Each group has its inner counterpart.
2. This inner counterpart is a completed whole. The outer results are still only partial.
3. These ten inner groups, forming one group, are related to the ashrams of the Masters and are each of them expressive of or governed by ten laws, embodying the controlling factors in group work. A law is an expression or manifestation of force applied, under the power of thought, by a thinker or group of thinkers.
4. These ten inner groups, embodying ten types of force and working synthetically to express ten laws, are an effort to bring in new and different conditions, and hence produce a new and better civilization. The Aquarian Age will see consummation.
5. The outer groups are a tentative and experimental effort to see how far humanity is ready for such an endeavour. [31]

The final sentence is another of D.K.'s statements which, in effect, say, 'It's up to you, brothers,' and consequently throw the ball firmly into the reader's court. Admittedly, there is a great deal of material on self-training scattered throughout A.A.B.'s writings, but it cannot be picked up all that easily. So many people have told me that they are interested in what is being written about but that they find the books themselves extremely difficult to assimilate. The whole style militates against superficial reading: one has to read the pasages back and forth and often go back to the beginning of a sentence before one has come to the end of it. There are qualifications, provisos and endless subheadings. People are forced to ponder and reflect and reconsider the whole subject matter, without making a snap judgement, as illustrated by the famous story of those twice-printed pages in *A Treatise on White Magic* which went unnoticed for two years.

The list of the particular seed-groups we are discussing can be found, with comments, in the course of D.K.'s lengthy discussion, in Volume 2 of *A Treatise on the Seven Rays*, of certain 'soul laws'. The terms used are much the same as those used in the description of them given for his students in the discipleship group. In the former case they are bracketed with what he calls 'the Law of Group Progress', which is concerned with particular influences that assist groups of souls engaged in elevating life on earth. Moreover, nearly forty pages at the beginning of *The Externalization of the Hierarchy* are given over to a more detailed discussion of the individual group tasks and functions. The whole subject is one of the less abstract and transcendental matters dealt with by D.K. because, as the groups' objectives indicate, it is concerned with the anchoring of progressive, creative energy right here on earth, as well as with raising the level of men's everyday existence so that a more genuinely wholesome, in every sense of the word, lifestyle is possible.

I suppose the best thing I can do is to give the evocative titles D.K. has chosen for each group and then very speedily pick one or, at the most, two of the sentences with which he begins to describe the functions he foresaw as being part of their development. The groups are nine in number, with a synthesizing and inclusive group intended to be built up with representatives from all the others. The information included now will provide a summary, but anyone really interested in following up the opportunities envisaged will need to do some research on his own account.

1. *Telepathic Communicators.* These people are receptive to impression from the Masters and from each other; they are the custodians of group purpose and, therefore, closely related to all the other types of groups . . .

2. *Trained Observers.* Their objective is to see clearly through all events, through space and time by means of the cultivation and use of the intuition . . .

3. *Magnetic Healers.* They work intelligently with the vital force of the etheric body. The work to be done is that of the intelligent transmission of energy to various parts of the nature — mental, emotional and physical . . .

4. *Educators of the New Age.* Their service is along the line of culture and they will work to bring in the new type of education. Their emphasis will be upon the building of the antahkarana and upon the use of the mind in meditation . . .

5. *Political Organizers.* They will work in the world of human government, dealing with the problems of civilization and with the relationships existing between nations. The bringing about of international understanding will be their major objective . . .

6. *The Workers in the Field of Religion.* Their work is to formulate the universal platform of the new world religion. It is a work of loving synthesis and it will emphasize the unity and the fellowship of the spirit . . .

7. *The Scientific Servers.* They will reveal the essential spirituality of all scientific work which is motivated by love of humanity and its welfare, which relates science and religion and brings to light the glory of God through the medium of His tangible world and His works . . .

8. *Psychologists.* Their major task will be to relate, through approved techniques, the soul and the personality, leading to the revelation of divinity through the medium of humanity. They will act also as transmitters of illumination between groups of thinkers and as illuminators of group thought . . .

9. *Financiers and Economists.* They will work with the energies and forces which express themselves through the interchange and the values of commerce; they will deal with the Law of Supply and Demand and with the great principle of *Sharing* which ever governs divine purpose . . .

10. *Creative Workers.* They link and blend life and form creatively. Their work is also largely philosophical and concerned with the task of relating — factually and scientifically — the other nine types of groups so that they may work creatively upon the physical plane and the divine plan may clearly appear as a result of this synthesis which they bring about. [32]

I wrote earlier about the technique for working 'as if'. D.K. writes 'as if' the groups are already here, as presumably they are as far as that which he calls the 'inner counterparts' are concerned. Only the first four seem to have been started in embryo amongst his own students, so once again it is left to us to prove the Hermetic principle that as it is above, so it can be below.

A few people who have studied the books in which the above descriptions appear have naturally enough tried to experiment. An international network of an ecumenical nature calling itself the Meditation Group for the New Age is amongst these; it follows a programme of creative reflection on laws and principles which D.K. indicated could, if observed, help bring about the Kingdom of God. At a certain stage in this work a consideration of these groups becomes optional; the focus is merely a meditative one, adopted in order to provide an atmosphere in which they might flourish. Other, smaller, groups have focused on the subject in their own ways, and these experiments continue.

Meanwhile, within the planetary field of endeavour inhabited by intelligent men and women of goodwill, it must be clear that seed-groups, pattern-makers and specialized networks are coming into existence all the time, with or without the intercessory work of D.K. or anybody else. Some groups are feeling their way; others have a clear vision of their objectives and *raison d'être*, and among these some definitely seem to come under the umbrella of one or other of the chosen areas of influence. Whether or not they feel inspired from within I would not care to say. Synthesizing groups which may well contain several elements of the nine within them appear to be on the increase. In addition, there are obviously occasions such as specialized conferences when seed-groups or working-parties form from the assembly. These may coalesce for only a limited period but nonetheless produce a valuable impact. Of its very nature, a seed-group is hardly expected to retain the same appearance indefinitely; it is, after all, presumed to be part of a growth movement. It would be invidious to attempt to list examples, though we may mention one or two activities by way of illustration in the next chapter. In any case, whole directories of New Age groups, larger than this volume, are now being produced with increasing frequency and are not considered beneath the dignity of the best publishers.

It is natural that seed-groups should pop up in all shapes and sizes; however, in a close appraisal of the pattern-making potential of D.K.'s proposed groups a distinctive format emerges, and it is relevant to enquire why this should be so. The subject has been of some continuing interest to me because of the significance these particular seed-groups have for the future. What follows immediately is the roughest outline sketch of a little of the material that has turned up. Others may have taken their research much further, but in my opinion these concepts, though often couched in metaphorical terms, seem to offer some clues on how to proceed in a practical way.

D.K.'s material on this pattern came through in the 1930s, after the pronouncement on the New Group of World Servers, and it was during 1937 and 1938 that he tried to establish the groups amongst his own students. As just stated, the indications[33] are that only the first four were ever set up before the difficulties of world conflict made contact with some of the students a problem for A.A.B. An indication of a format for their structure is to be found in the fact that there are nine groups with a synthesizing tenth; this last group would contain a total of twenty-seven members, three representatives being drawn from each of the nine. Although this is hardly the place for a dissertation on the qualities of numbers, all numbers do have their individual qualities and properties and the significance of nine should be explored in this particular connection. It appears to be a linking, grounding, relating number, ideally suited to organisms designed to assist in the earthing of new energy. And not only are nine groups the visioned pattern, but the ideal geometry of each group would provide for a membership of nine contributors. Let us commence with the esoteric factors outlined in a variety of places throughout A.A.B.'s writings:

1. What could be called the machinery of man is related as being threefold at three levels: spirit, soul, and body. [34]
2. The same can be said of the causal vehicle or lotus of the soul as it is sometimes referred to, because of the flower-like design of its energy, emblematic of three tiers of three flame-like petals which gradually unfold through the experiences of knowledge, love and sacrifice. [35]
3. Nine initiations or particular expansions of consciousness provide the transmuting ladder from this sphere of existence into a wider cosmic life. [36] (see Appendix C).

Furthermore, we read in *A Treatise on the Seven Rays*, Volume V that '7 is the number of man, 8 is the number of the Hierarchy, and 9 is the number of initiation or of Shamballa'.

In discussing those suitable for this type of group effort, D.K. states that the worker:

must have the heart centre awakened, and be so outgoing in his 'behaviour' that the heart is rapidly linked up with the heart centres of at least eight other people. Groups of nine awakened aspirants can then be occultly absorbed in the heart centre of the planetary Logos. Through it, His life can flow and the group members can contribute their quota of energy to the life influences circulating throughout His body. [37]

This type of information is by no means exclusive to D.K. If we look at certain myths, let alone ancient religious practices, which preserve many of nature's deep essential psychological, psychical and physical forces from the narrowing grasp of sectarian lines of thought, we find hints concerning the function of the nine pattern:

1. Nine Muses bring inspiration to mankind: a contribution

we usually attribute to ancient Greece, though its origins are more universal.

2. Nine Valkyrie maidens (daughters of the God King and the Earth Mother) carry heroes to Valhalla, in the Norse tradition.

3. An Indian legend claims that nine invisible men write, and rewrite, the books which give direction to human destiny.

4. Only in the ninth year of Bardic training were the words of power divulged, according to Welsh lore.

5. Nine golden apples on a silver bough made sweet music to draw the Celtic King Cormac to the palace of the sea God.

6. The body itself is seen by some as a symbolic city of nine gates or orifices, with the tenth opening as the 'brahmarandra' centre on the crown. (The tonsure of the monk, like the crown of kings and pontiffs, can be seen as emblematic of this state of opened awareness.)

The passageway or relationship between heaven and earth is always involved, and creativity, as a means of transition or a way through, is frequently involved as well. This is not dissimilar to Mircea Eliade's summary which we looked at in relation to the antahkarana. However, such is the impress of this particular pattern that the spells, charms, curses and exhortations of old often required a ritual involving the triple three in order to be effective.[38] D.K.'s pattern-groups may be intended for new purposes and a rejuvenating cycle of spiritual impact upon the earth, but the format he has adopted is exceedingly ancient in its function and usage. A recent film[39] built part of its story around the statement that a configuration of nine is part of the basic structure of substance in which life on earth is grounded. The sacred kingdom of Shamballa,[40] the Father's House or Source for manifestation on our planet, is depicted in Tibetan yogic tradition as a land guarded by snow mountains and divided into eight kingdoms, with a central palace or kingdom for the king, again protected by mighty peaks. Speculative, factual and transcendental instances of this are no doubt plentiful, but even without such support, nine remains a useful number of people for a small working group or a committee. The Baha'i faith is an example of a religious order which uses this structure for their governing, guiding committees.

It is an extremely mobile pattern and applies itself quite neatly to a number of 'systems' of philosophical thought. This is not the place to explore this in any great detail, though it may be of interest to readers to research this, and a couple of instances will give the experts something to ponder. For example, an application to the Sephiroth or Tree of Life of Jewish mysticism and Hermetic thought could be set up as:

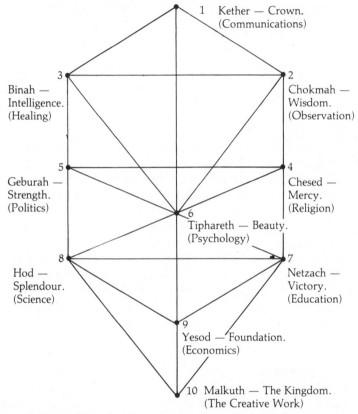

1 Kether — Crown.
(Communications)

3 Binah — Intelligence.
(Healing)

2 Chokmah — Wisdom.
(Observation)

5 Geburah — Strength.
(Politics)

4 Chesed — Mercy.
(Religion)

6 Tiphareth — Beauty.
(Psychology)

8 Hod — Splendour.
(Science)

7 Netzach — Victory.
(Education)

9 Yesod — Foundation.
(Economics)

10 Malkuth — The Kingdom.
(The Creative Work)

(It is also interesting that in a fourfold Tree representing the four realms in relationship — where Da'ath, the hidden station or Abyss, situated in the upper square, is found to be the Kingdom of the realm above — the pillars on either side will have nine temples or stations.[41])

The enneagram ('the symbol of self-sustained evolution or transformation'[42]) could doubtless offer several permutations. Using a straightforward circular motion — if one may be so paradoxical — the emergence of the groups could be read like this:

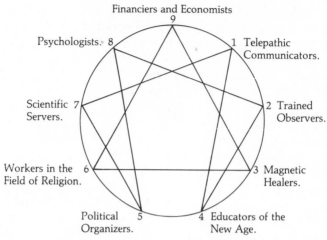

I myself would consider that an experiment with the first three (communicators, observers and healers) forming the triangle (3-6-9), would prove interesting. Their function gives them a kind of guiding role in relation to the areas of mind, emotion and vitality so that their work can clear the atmosphere and set the scene wherein the other more objective activities can operate effectively.

Yet it is perhaps by going back to the Egyptian cosmological ennead[43] that we can really derive a clue to the redemptive nature of the tenth group, which D.K. hardly discussed at all except to say that when the representatives of all the other groups were 'in rapport with each other, there should come to all the groups such a quickening of their life that they will become one living, vibrant organism'.[44]

It is for this reason I find the old Baconian word 'organon', derived from the same root as 'organic' and 'organization', a suitable title for these enneagrammatic seed-groups. If we consider the dictionary's[45] definition of an organon as 'an instrument of thought', the choice of this word to designate groups that are channels for consciousness seems entirely appropriate. Consider the diagram shown on page 119. In the materialization of the four principles, duality is manifest within the ennead, but from Isis springs Horus, the directing eye, who, with his consort Hathor, goddess of beauty and succour of the dead, can offer resurrection and return. John Anthony West writes in *Serpent in the Sky*:

The Grand Ennead emanates from the Absolute, or 'central fire' (in the terminology of Pythagoras). The nine Neters (Principles) circumscribed about One (The Absolute) becomes both One and Ten. This is the symbolic analog of the original Unity; it is repetition, the return to the source. In Egyptian mythology the process is symbolized by Horus, the Divine Son.[46]

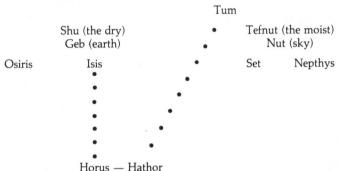

The Pythagorean tetractys (also discussed by Mr West), pictured like a triangle of nine points, with the tenth at the centre and containing within itself the keys to harmony, provides another example of the same concept. Those who feel themselves linked to A.A.B.'s lineage of spiritual work may here find a clue to one of the reasons why her own teacher, whom we have not discussed, is a motivator and inspirer of this particular kind of group work.

D.K.'s teaching seems at first glance to offer a distinctly male-oriented Lodge, and little teaching is given on the Taras, which are discussed by Helena Roerich.[47] Nevertheless, he does discuss the phrase 'the Mother of the World'[48] and remarks that, when the huge deva or angelic hierarchical evolution is taken into account, our planet is currently manifesting a female aspect. There is also mention of Lilith, allegedly one of the great Atlantean goddesses.[49] And in relation to the astrology of form, there is an intriguingly short discussion of 'our lady the moon' in relation to celestial forces with female names.

Be all that as it may, what we might call the Isis factor within the ennead/organon/pattern-group, resulting in the nurturing of the child, the project, the group purpose, the new day, is something that seems to be going on now through the patient, reflective work on the 'patterns' undertaken by such networks as the Meditation Group for the New Age; though, naturally, this is only a stage on the way to the emergence of such groups into the greater objectivity of Horus-like endeavour and triumphant effort. This later phase invites the attention of those whose courage may be roused by the prospect.

D.K.'s recognition of all this is hinted at (and as he often explained, a hint is all he is prepared to give) in the esoteric teaching given on the astrological sign Virgo, the Virgin:

Virgo is definitely related, through the medium of the various planetary rulers, to eight other signs of the zodiac and it is, therefore, with these eight signs that we are concerned because they produce an inter-related synthesis of nine signs (including Virgo). In this inter-related numerical synthesis and fruitful inter-relation lies hid the entire history of human progress and the secret of the process of divine manifestation . . . The relation of Virgo to eight signs . . . and the nine potencies play their part in developing the Christ life in the individual and in the mass of men. [50]

We have said nothing about the immense tract of teaching D.K. gave on astrology, a subject which he designated the most occult science. [51] (A hundred books could lose their way there; this small volume would not stand a chance.) Aries, Gemini, Taurus, Cancer, Scorpio, Sagittarius, Aquarius and Pisces are the constellations referred to above.

Much of the material produced by Mrs Roerich on the Mother of the World has been collected from her various writings and published as a booklet of that name, available from the Agni Yoga Society. Legend has it that after the Atlantean debacle those representing whatever aspect of the hierarchical Lodge was then in incarnation retreated from public view [52] (though there were positive reasons for this, related to their own development) and the great Goddess 'veiled her face'. Now, however, as the Lodge prepares to take a more active role in worldly organization, the feminine aspect will also manifest in new ways. There may be some who feel they can see this symbolically expressed in current social events, as women strive to play a more prominent role in many areas. Tibetan legend holds that the Mother's emissaries can be the best guides to Shamballa, the Holy City. In a recent book, *The Way to Shambhala*, Edwin Bernbaum, who undertook research on the subject while working for the Peace Corps in Nepal, records the dream of a lama who is guided to Shamballa by the saviouress with seven eyes, the White Tara or female Bodhisattva.[53]

This book goes into the legend of Shamballa quite deeply from the point of view of Tibetan religious doctrine and then looks at it in the sense of its being a mystical and psychological analogy that is considerably appropriate to our times. In later chapters, the author examines the myth of the journey to Shamballa in a way that would be quite familiar to those who favour the type of 'guided daydream' exercise that is much used by contemporary transpersonal psychologists as a means of exploring consciousness. This particular group of legends depicts the world as being engulfed by barbarism, with the king of Shamballa even sharing his throne with the barbarian monarch until the latter goes too far, makes a bid for supreme power and is slaughtered in a great battle. Through this, and indeed through the fact that the barbarians had been the ones chiefly responsible for precipitating the conflict, the open rule of Shamballa is established throughout the world, which consequently becomes an extension of its blessed domain. One is led to believe that there is great speculation amongst certain Tibetan scholars about the period of history wherein the battle is to take place. Perhaps, at different levels, it is a recurring event and is to some extent always taking place. Mr Bernbaum cites the Book of Revelations, the *Iliad* and the *Mahabharata* as illustrations of the way in which the pattern this sort of great myth exemplifies, can take hold of human consciousness. The author questions whether the misapplication of Western material technology is part of it. Certainly, Tibetans might look at the cultural destruction undertaken by the Red Guard element from China and wonder whether the moment had not already arrived, and whether the compensating wisdom of the King can flower in the emptiness thus created.

D.K. wrote a great deal on the subject of Shamballa, and it was an interesting case of synchronicity when Karma Samten wrote to me about Mr Bernbaum's book while I was assembling this material, because D.K. in fact asked one of his students to write a book of a similar title in the 1940s. He suggested a great many things to his students, of course, but this particular item will serve well as an illustration because of the centrality of the theme. History shows that the book in question did not get written at that time, and in 1946 we find D.K. writing:

The call went out to you from the ashram to write upon the theme of Shamballa, the centre where the will of God is known and from where the love of God flows forth . . . As you considered the theme of Shamballa (and later rejected my suggestion to write upon it) you brought yourself in contact with the energy emanating from Shamballa. Yet, my brother, had you occupied yourself with my suggestion and dealt with the theme *The Way into Shamballa* much of that Shamballa force would have been transmuted along constructive lines and creative endeavour. [54]

Again we must reflect that this is now 'water passed under the bridge'. Mr Bernbaum has picked up this universal theme in his own way, and the public is consequently indebted to him for an interesting and, whether or not it is immediately recognized as such, a timely book.

Three years before D.K. wrote the above, he gave his 'co-disciple, beloved brother and my friend', as he addressed his recipient, six statements on Shamballa with which to germinate his work:

1. Shamballa is the place of purpose. It is a purpose which cannot be understood until the Plan is followed. Herein lies a clue.
2. Shamballa is not a Way, but a major centre of related states and a relatively static energy — energy held ready for creative purposes by the focused intention of the Great Council, acting under the directing eye of the Lord of the World.
3. Shamballa is the major point of tension upon the planet. It is a tension that expresses loving intelligent will, free from all self-will or mental bias.
4. Shamballa is the major receptive agent upon the planet, from the angle of solar inflow, but at the same time it is the main distributing point of energy, from the angle of the kingdoms in nature, including the fifth kingdom. From the point of tension the life pattern of the planetary Logos and His will become embodied and finally matured through the processes of evolution.
5. Shamballa receives energy from various solar and extra-solar Entities or centres of emphatic and energetic life; i.e., from Venus, from the Central Spiritual Sun, from the current conditioning constellation through which our sun may be passing, from the Great Bear and other cosmic centres. Sirius, so important a factor in the spiritual life of the planet, brings its energies to bear direct upon the Hierarchy, and energy from

Sirius does not normally enter our planetary life via Shamballa.

6. Shamballa is the head centre, speaking symbolically, of our planetary life, focusing will, love and intelligence in one great and fundamental Intention and holding that focused point throughout the entire life cycle of a planet. This great Intention embodies current purpose and expresses itself through the medium of the Plan. [55]

The chart in Appendix A (see page 175) illustrates D.K.'s idea of Shamballa in relation to the hierarchy of realized men and humanity as we know it. From his point of view, all are kingdoms in nature in their own right, each as different in its way as, we would judge, such subhuman kingdoms as the animal kingdom and the vegetable kingdom are from each other. Although all kingdoms contain varying degrees of sentient consciousness, each one, so far as we can tell, operates in a manner very different from that of its fellows.

The present Dalai Lama is reportedly convinced of Shamballa's material existence in this world. [56] The Ven. Chögyam Trungpa Rinpoche described it to me as a 'kind of garden of Eden' — a source point, if you like. There is, I believe, a legend that a former Mahochohan (Great Lord of Civilization) in far distant times, actually built a material city of Shamballa on 'the White Island'. D.K. mentions something of early history in *A Treatise on White Magic*:

Students of these mysteries need to remember that though Shamballa is spoken of as existing in physical matter and as occupying a definite location in space, the physical matter referred to is etheric, the Lord of the World and his assistants of the higher degrees occupying bodies formed of etheric matter.

It was decided about seventeen million years ago (the coming of the Hierarchy and the founding of Shamballa being about eighteen and a half million years ago) to have on the dense physical plane an organization and a headquarters for the mysteries, and to have a band of Adepts and Chohans who would function in dense physical bodies and thus meet the need of the rapidly awakening humanity.

The first outpost for the Shamballa Fraternity was the original temple of Ibez and it was located in the centre of South America, and one of its branches at a much later period was to be found in the ancient Mayan institutions, and the basic worship of the Sun as the source of life in the hearts of men. A second branch was later established in Asia, and of this branch the Himalayan and southern Indian adepts are the representatives, though the work is materially changed. At a later date than the present, discoveries will be made, revealing the reality of the old form of hierarchical work; ancient records and monuments will be revealed, some above ground and many in subterranean fastnesses. As the mysteries of Central Asia in the land stretching from Chaldea and Babylon through Turkestan to Manchuria, including the Gobi desert, are opened up, it is planned that much of the early history of the Ibezhan workers will be revealed.[57]

This is fairly straightforward, though other statements made by D.K. seem to be designed to be evocative of what Mr Bernbaum would call 'the inner mind'.

Enough, I believe, has been said to indicate that Shamballa, or whatever name we choose to give it, is the directing centre to which the Lodge A.A.B. had contact with looks for its own guidance. To us it remains a place of mystery, but that word 'mystery' in an old Greek scriptural translation[58] is interpreted as meaning 'the secret plan of the king'. Its king is 'the Ancient of Days, the Eternal Youth, the Lord of the World, Sanat Kumara, Melchizedek, the embodiment of the Planetary Logos',[59] all these being the graphic titles employed by D.K. in his effort to find a reference point to which we can respond. The Plan itself D.K. discusses throughout his teachings, and in one place he gives a most curious summary of it:

You might here ask and rightly so: What is the plan? When I speak of the plan I do not mean such a general one as the plan of evolution or the plan for humanity which we call by the somewhat unmeaning term of soul unfoldment. These two aspects of the scheme for our planet are taken for granted, and are but modes, processes and means to a specific end. The plan as at present sensed, and for which the Masters are steadily working, might be defined as follows: It is the production of a subjective synthesis in humanity and of a telepathic interplay which will eventually annihilate time. It will make available to every man the true significance of his mind and brain and make him the master of that equipment and will make him therefore omnipresent and eventually open the door to omniscience. This next development of the plan will produce in man an understanding — intelligent and co-operative — of the divine purpose for which the One in Whom we live and move and have our being has deemed it wise to submit to incarnation. Think not that I can tell you of the plan as it truly is.[60]

Poor A.A.B., with material like this to write; it was no wonder her detractors spoke of her as 'that peculiar lady with her ear to the keyhole of Shamballa'.[61] The phrase 'the eventual annihilation of time' is most mystifying and certainly grips the attention. What can it all mean? Wherever and whenever one may be, one pays one's dues to the past, lives for the present and prepares for the future — inevitably. As man struggles through sequential time, wobbles in cyclic time and is psychologically confused by his own sense of subjective time, he is forced into experiencing both *rajas* ('action') and *tamas* ('inertia') in order to discover *sattva* ('rhythm') and with it some degree of timeless equilibrium. Mr Bernbaum's book devotes a chapter to 'The Wheel of Time', the Kalacakra teachings reportedly given by the Lord of Shamballa 'to show people how to free their minds from the ignorance and illusion that cause their suffering'.[62] He sees the Kalacakra tantra as the pinnacle of Tibetan Buddhism.

D.K.'s writings agree that the essence of the esoteric teachings as well as the present spiritual push originally emanate from Shamballa.[63] He describes the Master Morya as overseeing esoteric schools truly preparing souls for 'ashramic contact and work', because the will aspect of human equipment is involved. And because of the first ray synthesizing power a contact through this ashram with Shamballa is maintained.[64] In this respect he fulfils the lineage role of Vajrapani, 'Bodhisattva of Power and Master of Secret Teaching', though in a more outward respect his ashram is deeply concerned with the attempted inspiration of international statesmen.[65]

D.K. offers the hope of three figurative doors into Shamballa and we can at least ponder them from a psychological point of view:

1. There is *the door of the reason*, of pure perception of truth. Christ gave the clue to this teaching when He said 'I am the Way, the Truth and the Life' . . .
2. There is *the door of the will*. This is a penetrating power which relates Plan to Purpose and which has in it the faculty of coherent persistence . . .
3. I can find no words to express the nature of the third door. Let us, in default of a better term, call it *the door of the monadic sense of essential duality*.[66]

The Way to Shambhala has a picture of the Tibetan symbol for the Ten of Power as an emblem of the Kalacakra. This seems to bring us back again to the nine (plus one for wholeness) pattern-groups. I would humbly suggest that these seem to be a more immediately practical entrance to 'the journey' for most active, intelligent men and women of goodwill who, while 'looking to the hills, from whence cometh their help', wish to do something about transforming the place in which they now find themselves:

Two thousand years have gone since Gethsemane and since Christ made His initial contact with the Shamballa force and by this means, and on behalf of humanity, established a relationship which even at the close of twenty centuries is but a thin frail line of connecting energy.

This Shamballa force is nevertheless available for right usage but the power to express it lies in its understanding (as far as may be possible at this midway point in human evolution) and its *group* use. It is a unifying, synthetic force, but can be used as a regimenting, standardizing force. May I repeat those two key words to the use of the Shamballa energy: Group Use and Understanding. [67]

Just in case the reader has become dismayed and bewildered by such a mass of esoteric and somewhat abstruse material, it may act as encouragement — or perhaps as ballast — to know that D.K., when writing to his brother and student, whose interest in Shamballa he sought to encourage, time and time again stressed the factor of simplification. In the midst of all his teaching on Shamballa, he gave a seed-thought on which to ruminate: 'The simplicity of the soul opens the Way to Shamballa.' [68] And if you analyse it, we have at root discussed nothing very complex:

1. People of goodwill can strengthen their intentions by joining with their companions in service.
2. By adopting some of the deep, essential patterns of nature, these groups can in turn strengthen their capacity to channel energy.
3. And the flow of energy ('the saving Shamballa force' [69]) can carry consciousness to the heart of life itself.

Perhaps we should borrow the closing word on this rather extraordinary prospect from the poet T.S. Eliot, who in the last of his *Four Quartets*, speaks of:

A condition of complete simplicity
(Costing not less than everything) [70]

The Affirmation of the Disciple

I am a point of light within a greater Light.
I am a strand of loving energy within the stream of Love divine.
I am a spark of sacrificial Fire, focused within the fiery Will of God.
And thus I stand.

I am a way by which men may achieve.
I am a source of strength, enabling them to stand.
I am a beam of light, shining upon their way.
And thus I stand.

And standing thus, revolve
And tread this way the ways of men,
And know the ways of God.
And thus I stand. [71]

5. 'The Ajna Centre of the World'[1]

In discussing the speed at which transformation can take place through the individual or in the world, D.K. once remarked on the need for the soul to register 'the strength of the Timeless One and the persistence of the One Who is from the beginning'.[2] In this respect, he stated, the relation between cause and effect could be spontaneous and simultaneous rather than gradual and sequential. Possibly this concept is an aspect of the ancient teachings of the Kalacakra or the Wheel of Time which emanate from Shamballa and also in some measure belong to those visions of transformation within the human world which tantalize the aspirations of so many people. Discussing the nature of time, D.K. states that it is 'related to the will aspect and is dependent upon the dynamic life, self-directed, which produces persistence and which demonstrates persistence in that dynamic focus of intention by periodic or cyclic appearance.'[3] Elsewhere, he writes: 'The vibratory process necessitated by the utilization of the form, this we call Time, whether in connection with a man, a planetary Logos, or the Deity.'[4] This seems to concern the development of relationship in manifestation and therefore conditions activity throughout nature, for further on in the same place we read:

We might therefore consider *time* as that process of activity or that progression in development, wherein the indwelling consciousness is seeking its opposite, and coming under the Law of Attraction, which leads to atomic, human, planetary, spiritual, solar and cosmic marriage.

Throughout A.A.B.'s work and the teaching expounded in her books, and especially where anything to do with practical world affairs or outward-going service is concerned, there is an effort to train people to work in rhythmical cycles.[5] Approached from a rather subjective point of view, this could be seen as an almost athletic approach to the whole enterprise. We have already mentioned, albeit briefly, the value of studying the cycles of inhalation and exhalation with moments of interlude in between that are familiar to practitioners of pranayama yogic exercises. [6] We have, equally briefly, looked at the solar rhythm recorded by the phases of the moon. [7] Besides these there exist many other, much larger, subtle and energetic tides and cycles, hinted at by D.K. and available for man's attention. It is interesting to note, in connection with the fifth of D.K.'s six statements on Shamballa (see the last chapter) that according to Robert Temple, who conducted research into their customs with respect to beliefs about Sirius, [8] the Dogon tribe of Central Africa have, in addition to their agrarian lunar calendar, three liturgical ones relating to that particular star, the sun and Venus. It has to be considered, I think, that as far as our present society is concerned a great deal that is referred to in A.A.B.'s writings is really knowledge which we have either carelessly mislaid or had taken from us by events and into which we are now being urged to make a penetrating investigation.

In a letter to one of his students, and when discussing the particular rhythm of effort that was applicable to that subjective, composite grouping referred to by him as 'the New Group of World Servers', D.K. expanded on the subject of cycles as follows:

Forget not, all creative processes proceed with a cyclic rhythm. The rhythm set by the New Group of World Servers is a three-year cycle and to this rhythm you will find yourself conforming. The end of one such cycle came in May 1936 . . . The keynote of the first year's work is consolidation, that of the second year must be expansion whilst the keynote of the third year must be the making of a definite impact upon the public consciousness, by the sounding and the emphasizing of some one clear note. If this cyclic measure is kept thus in mind, no serious mistakes will be made . . . This cyclic rhythm will release from strain and yet enable the workers in the Group to feel there is no failure. It is impossible to do good work where a sense of failure or lack of attainment is found. [9]

Perhaps this application of cyclic activity through the said world-wide subjective networking of servers can provide the cue for us to make a more thorough investigation of the group and its constitution. A.A.B. referred to the announcement of the group's existence in 1932 as 'epoch-making in its significance', and in the terms in which she appears to have been thinking that 'significance' extended far beyond the relatively small sphere of theosophical aspirants and allied investigators. In order to be of real use, this application has to be planetary, and indeed the objectives of the group in immediate human terms are given as *The raising of the level of human consciousness . . .* so that intelligent thinking men and women will be consciously in touch with the world of ideas and the realm of intuitive perception. *The clarifying of the international situation;* and, *the growth of the group idea.'* [10]

The last aim clearly connects quite closely with the establishment of the pattern-groups previously mentioned but is obviously not dependent upon them. All manner of groupings are possible and can be made useful as men and women of goodwill organize themselves for action in the directions they consider worth while. When and where the Ennead-like organons envisaged by D.K. can be brought into being, these can perform their specialized functions rather like life-carrying enzymes; their catalytic influence would circulate within the whole corporate network of New Group activity, strengthening and enhancing it. However, as the given explanations of the pervasive New Group indicate, its world work is already well under way, with or without 'special vitamins':

All true servers everywhere belong to the New Group of World Servers, whether their line of service is cultural, political, scientific, religious, philosophical, psychological or financial. They constitute part of the inner group of workers for humanity, and of the world mystics, whether they know it or not.

This group gives to the word 'spiritual' a wide significance; they believe it to mean an inclusive endeavour towards human betterment, uplift and understanding; the give it the connotation of tolerance, international synthetic communion, religious inclusiveness, and of all trends of thought which concern the integrating development of the human being.

It is a group therefore without a terminology or bible of any kind; it has no creed nor any dogmatic formulations of truth. The motivating impulse of each and all is love of God as it works out in love, for one's fellowmen. [11]

The New Group of World Servers are the people who are building the new world order. They are all of them definitely serving humanity and are, through the power of their response to the spiritual opportunity, tide and note, emerging out of every class, group, church, party, race and nation, and are therefore truly representative. They speak all languages; they embrace all religions, all sciences and all philosophies. Their characteristics are synthesis, inclusiveness, intellectuality, and fine mental development. They say nothing and write no word which could feed the fires of hatred and thus tend to separate man from man and nation from nation. They own to no creed, save the creed of Brotherhood, based on the One Life. They recognize no authority save that of their own souls. They make no clamour about their own ideas, discoveries and theories, but because they are so inclusive in their outlook and so wide in their interpretation of truth they see the hand of God in all happenings, His imprint upon all forms and His note sounding forth through every channel of communication between the subjective reality and the objective outer form. [12]

Quite a lot of the earliest material concerning this networking and its eventual effectiveness appeared in D.K.'s study of white magic, although when this script was transmitted the title 'New Group of World Servers' appears not to have been employed. [13] Apart from that, all that was written then and later carries the same themes of planetary synthesis and human brotherhood illuminated by a growing telepathic empathy amongst the visionaries of the world. No membership lists, no offices, no outward organization, no badges or time-consuming procedures; only, as Christ put it, by 'fruitage' or quality of work could these people be recognized — and some, I dare say, may be too busy to stop and recognize themselves. All the same, D.K. did say that they have a motto and that it means, whatever words are actually used: 'The Glory of the One'. [14]

The other skills listed [15] as being appropriate to members of the seed-groups of nine would appear to be applicable here too. The technical and dynamic capacity to link with the outgoing heart energy of 'at least eight other people' has already been recorded here, and I would imagine this to be a prerequisite of the New Group. Two further requirements are:

    a)   An awakening head centre which allows an ability to 'hold the mind steady in the light': a technical term referring to the power to illuminate the mind and the thinking processes with the light of the soul and to do this at will, at least to some degree. (All this is implied in the passage from the Patanjali yoga sutras discussed in Chapter 1.)

2. Next, the worker should have discovered a field, be it cultural, scientific, humanitarian, artistic, religious, philosophical, psychological or similar, in which creative skill is being usefully exercised.

If anything D.K.'s description of the general requirements for the New Group (grouped, as such things frequently are, in a group of three) seem less exacting than those technical abilities required by the living enneads; yet in a way they are more difficult:

How shall one qualify? The rules are simple, and three in number. First, learn to practise harmlessness; then desire nothing for the separated self; and thirdly, look for the sign of divinity in all. Three simple rules, but very hard to accomplish. [16]

He returned to the practice of harmlessness several times in his teaching, [17] and when one considers just how hard it is to be truly harmless in thought, word, deed and emotional reaction, one can appreciate the positive value of this injunction for all spiritual development. In a different wording, a similar concept is stressed in many teachings; for example, the contemporary metaphysical teaching expressed in *A Course in Miracles* sees forgiveness as a primary means of releasing spiritual happiness; [18] and in her book *Heart*, Helena Roerich terms vengeance a megaphone for the wrong it intends to avenge. [19] Once again, motive seems to be an important key, for the surgical removal of a malevolent influence can be motivated by a spontaneous surge of goodwill. D.K. stated categorically that he approached the practice of harmlessness 'with zest and understanding, for it is (if truly carried out) the destroyer of all limitation'. The two commandments of Christ, based upon love, are essentially embraced by the practice of harmlessness.

As one might expect, D.K. lists certain drawbacks which make co-operation with the New Group's aims difficult and unlikely:

I tell you with emphasis that four things only keep a man from affiliation.

First: an uncoordinated personality. This involves necessarily an untrained mind and a feeble intellect.

Second: a sense of separateness, of distinction, and of being set apart or different from one's fellow men.

Third: the possession of a creed. No matter how good a formula of beliefs it may be, it inevitably produces exclusiveness. It bars some out.

Fourth: pride and ambition. [20]

Here he has, incidentally, put his finger on one of the bugbears of esoteric movements down the years; and, incidentally, one of the probable reasons why so few esotericists, comparatively speaking, were to be found in the ranks of the New Group when he wrote about it.[21] This is the factor of exclusivity, of being different, knowing something the other poor boobies have not got wise to and so on, which produces some form of a 'holier than thou' effect. Knowledge there may be, but that is a technical matter and should lead to a greater responsibility and professionalism rather than an extravagant emotional reaction. Foster Bailey's effort in the 1950s was designed to bridge the gulf that sometimes appears because of this effect. The keynotes of what he judged important were encapsulated in a series of lectures later published as *Changing Esoteric Values*. Many others, under the pressure of the world scene which confronts us all, have responded to the same harmony of compassion and inclusive caring which animates the New Group and are designing their activities in accord with this spirit.

In this sense, the ambience or radiatory field of the New Group effect is the training ground for future world workers; it is the school *par excellence*. Anyone with a theory about what the world really needs can put himself forward and have his motives and project put through the fiery furnace of experience. The group bars no one who wants to put his capacity for love to the test; its need for caring scholars positively invites research and experiment. And at the end of each 'day of effort', a practical examination exercise will be available to all those wishing to take a look at their skill in action and volunteer an initiative in their self-chosen classroom.

Naturally enough, good work may also emerge via sources that require the personality razzmatazz of old-style ways. The conjunction of different energies can produce situations and crises which in themselves contain the energy of liberation; God is not left without witness in any circumstance. However, we read:

Know each of you for yourselves whether you stand for the new position, the new attitudes towards work, and for the subjective method. Decide once and for all whether you prefer to work in the old exoteric ambtious manner, building and vitalizing an organization, and so producing all the mechanism which goes with such a method of work. Remember that such groups are still greatly needed and are useful. It

is not yet the new age and the little ones must not be left exposed to
the new forces, nor turned out bereft of the nursery to which they
naturally belong.

Should the new mode of work appeal to you, see to it that the
personality is subordinated, that the life of meditation is kept paramount
in importance, that sensitivity to the subjective realm is cultivated, and
any necessary outer activities are handled from within outwards. Avoid
a purely mystical introspection or its opposite extreme, an over-
emphasized organizing spirit, remembering that a life of truly occult
meditation must inevitably produce outer happenings, but that these
objective results are produced by an inner growth and not by an outer
activity. An ancient Scripture teaches this truth in the following terms:

When the sun progresses into the mansion of the serving man, the
way of life takes the place of the way of work. Then the tree of life grows
until its branches shelter all the sons of men. The building of the Temple
and the carrying of the stones cease. The growing trees are seen; the
buildings disappear. Let the sun pass into its appointed place, and in
this day and generation attend ye to the roots of growth. [22]

This passage is, I believe, fairly crucial to an understanding of
the way A.A.B. chose to conduct her work and explains why,
to some, the consequences seem singularly undemonstrative in
outer organizational terms.

Some may well ask where are other instances of the 'presence'
of this New Group of World Servers? Given that it is primarily
a trend in consciousness, a collective of caring souls influencing
the outer scene subjectively, nonetheless there would have been
others besides A.A.B. who picked up the fact of the Group's
existence and delivered its message. I believe there are. The
number of people who recognize, through their own intuitive
perception, the reality of what the Group stands for is increasing
all the time; however, it is possible to instance a varied collection
of people who have been in the vanguard of those who articulated
the Group's principles in some original or creative way. To my
mind, a prime example is to be found in Teilhard de Chardin's
collected essays and lectures published under the title *Building
the Earth*. [23] His great call for the reorganization and regeneration
of human energy and his poetic vision for love, human unity and
research is of the essence of what the New Group labours to bring
into the light of day.

I do not doubt that each person reading this book will be able
to put his or her finger on at least a few activities that illustrate

the kind of influence we would suppose emanates from the New Group, without necessarily labelling the person or persons involved as part of the New Group (which would put them in an invidious position even if it were true). And, of course, in some instances they may be simply picking up the subjective tide which flows as a result of the Group work. There are, for example, many specialized networks which could be considered as a flowering of the ideas examined in the last two chapters, despite the fact that their originators may not necessarily have heard of A.A.B.'s activity.

One example that springs to mind is the Scientific and Medical Network, whose voluntary secretariat is based in the UK and whose membership is largely made up of qualified people who are earning or have at one time earned their livelihood by recognized scientific means and have therefore a proper training in objectivity. I mention them because, although they court no publicity, they have already been reported in the press. [24] Their careful and modest investigative work 'into paraphysical, parapsychological and spiritual matters and in action that might usefully flow from these' [25] certainly fulfils de Chardin's call for research. The London *Times* and *Sunday Times* [26] on one occasion reported their gatherings under such headlines as 'Clandestine Group of Doctors Meet' and 'The Network Comes out of Hiding'; however, the eminence of the speakers and supporters meant that the actual text gave an accurate rendering of the comments that were made. In considering this and other similar groups in different areas of work one would have to go far to equal Marilyn Ferguson's acclaimed review of this whole field of service, at least from an American or Western viewpoint, published under the title *The Aquarian Conspiracy*. [27] Many overtones of 'the New Group attitude' have been picked up by Miss Ferguson.

Yet it is not only in moral essay or investigative reporting that the Group is to be observed; the vision also makes itself apparent in creative invention. Ursula Le Guin's award-winning fantasy novel *The Left Hand of Darkness* contains a brief description of an inter-world association that echoes the New Group 'heart' quality. The quotations come from random remarks and explanations given by the association's one visiting representative on a planet that is being offered the chance of membership. Only one representative has been sent because, in this tale, two could

be considered an invasion and each world must decide for itself
in utter freedom, without any hint of coercion, whether or not
to join in:

The Ekumen is not a kingdom, but a co-ordinator, a clearing
house . . .
    The Ekumen doesn't rule, it co-ordinates. Its power is precisely the
power of its member states and worlds . . .
    It does not enforce laws; decisions are reached by council and consent,
not by consensus or command . . .
    The Ekumen is not essentially a government at all. It is an attempt
to reunify the mystical with the political, and as such is of course mostly
a failure; but its failure has done more good for humanity so far than
the successes of its predecessors. It has a society and it has, at least
potentially, a culture. It is a form of education; in one aspect it's a sort
of very large school — very large indeed. The motives of communication
and co-operation are of its essence, and therefore in another aspect it's
a league or union of worlds . . .
    Ekumen is our word; in the common tongue it's called the Household,
in yours it would be the Hearth. [28]

Many creative pronouncements capture or reflect aspects of the
New Group vision. Alexander Solzhenitsyn's 1970 Nobel prize
speech on the subject of literature, *One Word of Truth*, even
though he was not given the chance to deliver it orally is just
one such battle cry. [29] In the course of this text he takes the
opportunity to mention the United Nations Declaration of Human
Rights. [30] And perhaps one of the simplest and shortest
pronouncements — virtually a slip of paper that can be handed
to anyone — is His Holiness the fourteenth Dalai Lama's statement
The Principle of Universal Responsibility. One arresting sentence
in this simple document runs as follows: 'The rationale for
universal compassion is based on the simple principle of a spiritual
democracy.' And His Holiness continues:

    It is the recognition of the fact that every living being has an
equal right to, and desire for, happiness.'[31]

This raises the whole concept of Hierarchy, which can sometimes sound so authoritarian. It is a word D.K. uses more
often than not to describe the association of which the trans-
Himalayan Lodge is a part. It causes us to question why and how
Hierarchy is to be considered in relation to groups. It is in fact

because of the authoritarian connotation and the misunder-
standings that can ensue that I have chosen to use the term 'Lodge'
for our present reference, although I realize that this can also be
distasteful to some people. However, if they will make the effort
to consider their own prejudice against the term, they may find
that it is based on a fairly narrow interpretation of the word.
A working lodge, which is a form of group structure of whatever
variety, can hold within itself a functional structure or stairway
of responsibility — the Agni Yoga teachings[32] use the term 'a
chain of dynamos' — while at the same time allowing government
to proceed by mutual understanding of principle, consultation
and acclaim. Nonetheless, I imagine we would all agree that to
work effectively a Lodge would require a degree of clear vision
and identification with a large-scale common purpose, unless it
had settled for strictly limited objectives. Synchronizing deep
purpose and wide vision on the human scene can be a tricky
business.

Foster Bailey was responsible for another book entitled *The
Meaning of Masonry*, which examines this subject in the light
of D.K.'s ideas. In a discussion of landmarks we learn:

Masons also regard *the fact that all men are equal* as a landmark. All
start upon their search blinded and ignorant; all pass from stage to stage
and from test to test, as they progress towards the light; all are equal
in origin, in goal and in their innate divinity, for all are the children
of the same Father and all recognize the same God, and the fact that
they are brothers.[33]

This statement seems to accord quite well with the Dalai Lama's
thinking on this theme, although a Buddhist would naturally use
different insights to describe the theological concept of God the
Father.

There is no question in my mind that in A.A.B.'s sense of the
'New Group of World Servers' it can be regarded 'as a sort of
very large school — very large indeed'; certainly any effort to
fulfil its objectives is 'a form of education'. The present trustees
responsible for maintaining the Lucis Trust (which Foster Bailey
constructed to take care of A.A.B.'s work), under the presidency
of Mrs Mary Bailey, his second wife and co-worker, keep the
stated objectives of the New Group in the forefront of their minds
when reviewing policy. As I understand it, the hope is that friends

Mrs Mary Bailey, Ian Gordon-Brown and Foster Bailey sitting at the door of the house on Broadwater Down, Tunbridge Wells, used by A.A.B. on her later visits to the U.K., and afterwards purchased by the Lucis Trust.

and students of the work may aid useful service activities that display the inclusive and constructive qualities of the New Group, wherever these may be found, either in an active state or in a germinating embryonic one.

I believe it is the hope of those interested in the production of this book that some indication should be given of how far this may have been successful. Clearly the evidence of New Group activity whenever it appears is some sort of vindication of A.A.B.'s teaching. Therefore the discovery of it, for those interested in what she had to say, is a serious matter. But seriousness can be a very private thing, and the choice of effective lines of service is a highly individual concern. In a newspaper article, the economist E.F. Schumacher showed how this is true:

Men always seem to need at least two things simultaneously that, on the face of it, seem to be incompatible. We always need both freedom and order. We need the freedom of lots and lots of small, autonomous units, and, at the same time, the orderliness of large — possibly global — unity and co-ordination. When it comes to action, we obviously need small units, because action is a highly personal affair, and one cannot be in touch with more than a very limited number of persons at any one time. But when it comes to the world of ideas, to principles or to ethics, to the indivisibility of peace and also of ecology, we need to recognize the unity of mankind and base our actions upon this recognition. [34]

As thousands of people have read Mrs Bailey's books and thousands of these thousands have, over the intervening years since they were written, passed through at least some of the Arcane School course, fusing and blending the ideas they found there with all the other concepts that come into their lives, not to mention the karmic conditioning that was or is their lot, it is quite impossible to make a just assessment of the fruitage. Added to that is the fact of inviolate confidentiality. Individual students may find it politic to work in silence. The fact that they meditate and study esoteric books from time to time may not be a useful advertisement for their day-to-day objectives. In any event, the school does not divulge its membership; I do not know its current state and have not enquired.

Foster Bailey discussed the subject of secrecy, which upsets some people who feel that they are on occasion being denied a favour which is, in their opinion, a right. Inherently, perhaps it is, but maybe equality-in-essence requires that it be demonstrated through equality of understanding, responsibility and skill before men can 'open the door to omniscience' (whether by supercomputer or within themselves) as the Plan prognosticates: [35]

Another important landmark is to be found in the carefully *preserved secrets of Masonry* . . . the Mysteries were ever carried on under the protection of silence and secrecy . . . The Workings of the Lodge on High remains for us, the vast body of humanity, a secret mystery . . . The secrecy which evokes so much antagonism today in many quarters is not based today upon the fact that the Masonic Order possesses anything of a truly secret nature, or that it hides some knowledge which is hidden from the public. There is little that is not known today about the Masonic work, and nothing that cannot be discovered by anyone who diligently seeks it. But the principle of secrecy is here upheld inviolate . . . they are guarding a process and a form which will provide a true home for the Mysteries when restored to humanity, and will protect them from the intrusion of the profane . . . Christ Himself conformed to such a rule . . . He spoke to the profane in parables, but, with His disciples and initiates He spoke of the mysteries of the Kingdom of God . . . Masonry symbolizing as it does the inner mysteries of the kingdom, and looking forward to the time (foretold by Christ) when the initiates of the divine Mysteries 'will do greater work' than He did, emphasizes the need for the strictest secrecy. [36]

I do not wish to imply by this that the Arcane School has a masonic foundation, other than its allegiance to the Lodge on High; it is, quite simply, a fact that a measure of sacred silence surrounds all interior growth processes, and this is as true in the case of human beings as it is of other kingdoms in nature.

Nevertheless, one can perhaps mention, quite legitimately, one or two activities of people who have at some time or another been interested in the broad stream of the goodwill work, who have also found the Baileys' efforts stimulating and have gone on to do something constructive in their own way, according to their own lights and within the particular environment that life opened to them. This does not mean that they are part of the New Group or some sort of Baileyite (or students of any school of thought at all) or even interested in the concept of some kind of hierarchical Lodge. It means merely that they have a measure of concern about the human state, that they have taken such opportunities as life has afforded them and done something constructive about it, as any reader of this book can similarly do, should they wish to express goodwill in a practical way.

A good example of what I mean by this is a lady in America whose husband, a business advisor, had a heart attack. As their children were grown and flown, she decided she would be the breadwinner for a time in order to give him a breathing space in which to fully recover. As a former professional journalist, she looked around for suitable employment in their nearest large town. She found a job with a girl's college, which was young enough in its history not to have yet produced old girls willing to return and take on the alumnae office. Jeanne Pontius Rindge accepted this post, but having got back in harness, so to speak, found that her energies overflowed the perimeter of the work required. She began organizing extracurricular lectures and other activities, including the encouragement of some experimental work through a college faculty head. Although this college was run by Catholic nuns, its courageous principal saw no reason not to consider contemporary issues, and one early event was a public dialogue between a Catholic priest and a Zen Buddhist — an event the nuns attended carrying their bedroom pillows because, as they allegedly explained, Zen meditation was done on the floor and they wanted to participate properly. Other contemporary and unusual issues focused through lively people quickly put the programme of lectures, workshops and papers on the map. And 'Human Dimensions', as this particular examination of man's potential came to be called, emerged into the public domain. Eventually, with various well-known citizens of Buffalo in support, it left the college which had given it birth and for a number of years provided an interesting, timely and stimulating cycle of research, debate, exchange and communication.

Another wide-ranging educative activity is Planetary Citizens. This is a non-governmental organization that gradually came into being with the purpose of stressing the need for planetary synthesis in response to a particular speech in which U Thant, an outstanding Secretary-General of the United Nations Organization, highlighted the urgency of the world's problems. Amongst others who picked up this focus was Donald Keys, a respected observer of the UN scene, who subsequently became President of Planetary Citizens. Mr Keys recently launched via Planetary Citizens a far-reaching educational programme which seeks to involve many groups and networked individuals in a widespread debate on global problems of all kinds and on the means for their solution. The chosen name for this endeavour, launched at the start of the 1980s in New York with approximately a hundred supportive or participating groups, is Planetary Initiative for the World We Choose.

In an entirely different field of work, Ian Gordon-Brown, an industrial psychologist interested in the growth movement started transpersonal psychology weekend workshops with the help of a Jungian-inclined colleague, Barbara Somers. Based on ideas and exercises drawn from Assagioli, Maslow, Progoff and others, these were initially mainly for professional people. Such was the demand they created over a period of a few years without any advertising other than by word of mouth that, both these people — who are currently being followed by other colleagues and co-workers — had to give up their posts to work full time meeting the need that their experimental work had unearthed.

Another co-worker, Lily Cornford, who was for a long time a book-keeper, had to wait almost to the point of retirement before coming fully into her field of service. But once off the leash, so to speak, and having passed through a strenuous period of training, she became for a time a chairperson for the Radionic Association and subsequently launched another therapeutic healing service. The authoress and painter Vera Stanley Alder, a friend of A.A.B., has for many years maintained a World Union Fellowship which lays emphasis on man's guardianship of the planet throughout the kingdoms of nature. Another stalwart lady, currently well into her nineties, Mrs Florence Garrigue, who worked in Mrs Bailey's New York office, cares for the American side of the Meditation Group for the New Age and was responsible for establishing its spectacular United States centre at Meditation Mount, Ojai. Yet another one-time colleague of hers, Regina Keller, with Frank Hilton and others, founded a School for Esoteric Studies based on teachings taken from D.K.'s transmissions to A.A.B.

Meditation Mount, a centre in the Ojai Valley, California, founded by Mrs Florence Garrigue and a group of co-workers to promote creative meditation for a new age influenced by the laws and principles of the Kingdom of God.

One could go on; this is a brief mention, by way of illustration, of just a few of those who took the initiative and joined with co-workers to found some useful group activity in line with a need, as they saw it, in human welfare and development. The point in mentioning them at all is to show that no extraordinary revelation or earth-shattering event is required to release the creative thread of the antahkarana. (Anyway, as A.A.B. stated almost jocularly during the conference held for Arcane School students on her final visit to the United Kingdom, those who receive revelations put themselves in a dangerous and difficult position.) Self-initiated effort may, like fishing, take some casts of one's line over the environmental flow before a response is felt, but in this respect people can take comfort from Christ's own advice to the fishermen. [37]

It is all an interwoven tapestry composed of a multitude of threads. There are the many autonomous groups that Schumacher clearly saw the need for, but there is also, high above them and illuminating them, according to A.A.B., the global vision. It was because of this interrelating factor and the need for interaction between vision and groups that D.K. and the Baileys placed emphasis on the dynamic of the goodwill work and the awakening of intelligent men and women of goodwill. D.K. explains [38] that the magnetism holding all in right relationship is empowered by 'the element of will and of an expressing purpose', which leads us back to the Divine Will or 'Shamballa force'. He illustrates his explanations with a quotation from the 'Old Commentary' (a source of Lodge teaching, often quoted by D.K.), which poetically describes this energy as:

a point of focused fire, found in the centre of the jewel. It stirs to life the quality of love which permeates the Ashram of the Lord. Radiation then can penetrate to other centres and to other lives, and thus the Lord is served.

Then in his usual way, he lists the functions of 'this magnetizing potency, this dynamic and energizing will':

1. It is the connecting energy which comes from Shamballa and 'enlivens' (literally and occultly understood) the Ashram of Sanat Kumara. It is, in one sense, the higher correspondence to the prana which 'enlivens' the dense physical body of man.

2.   It is the stimulating factor which produces cohesion among the various Ashrams, and is one of the sources of hierarchical unity. Putting it in other words, it is the service of the Plan which binds the seven Ashrams, with their subsidiary Ashrams, coherently into the one great Ashram. The Plan is the expression of the Purpose or the Will of God.

3.   This Shamballic magnetism not only relates the Ashrams to each other, but it is also the potency which evokes the will or the first ray nature inherent in every man but which is only consciously and definitely unfolded within the periphery of the great Ashram. [39]

The structure of the households within the House is, we learn, a functional one. There is but one ashram, [40] though many mansions or operative guilds, as, long ago, Christ said was the case. [41] Some ashrams, we are told, are yet in embryo awaiting the organizing lives that will awaken their sphere of work; others, such as the major ashrams upon the seven rays (see Appendix 3) appear to be in the full flower of their specialized service. [42] Yet none is really 'above' the others; each of the forty-nine fires has its own special significance. It would seem nevertheless that the degree of relationship into which all are drawn through contact with the Shamballa force has made possible the emergence of the New Group of World Servers, which in turn heralds the chance for men to civilize themselves upon a planetary scale.

The government of the whole interrelated organism of hierarchy, of the multifaceted lodge, is seemingly one of function or work assignment, if you like. Though in this respect, we would suppose the assignment echoes Kahlil Gibran's definition that 'work is love made visible'. [43] It is reportedly an appropriation of tasks taking place under the guidance of the Steersmen (the Greek word for which name is said by Norbert Weiner to have given rise to our modern term 'cybernetics' [44]) of the three departments or triune aspects of life, consciousness and creativity, and comes about through developed abilities to respond to qualified energies, which are hard for us to comprehend. [45] In any event let us repeat that part of the operation which could concern us most immediately. The degree of relationship (as a new factor in the evolution of consciousness) into which the united ashrams have been drawn and their increasing contact with the saving force of Shamballa have made possible the emergence of the New Group of World Servers as a functioning factor in the human race; and this in turn offers a chance for men to develop themselves in unity and achieve a truly global civilization. Are we up to the mark in identifying with such a goal?

In discussing identification, D.K. and A.A.B. seem almost to struggle with words in order to convey some element of this phase in man's potentially magnificent destiny:

Identification (to use the only word available for our purpose) is connected with dynamic life, with conscious enhancement, with completion and with creative sharing, plus process . . . It is connected with the circulation of that 'life more abundantly' to which the Christ referred when dealing with the true nature of His mission. It might be said that as He uttered this phrase this mission dawned on Him and He made a preliminary effort to serve Shamballa, instead of the Hierarchy of which He was even then the Head. Later, He enunciated as best He could the extent of this realization, in the words so familiar to Christians, 'I and My Father are One'. This He also attempted to elucidate in the seventeenth chapter of St. John's Gospel. There is no other passage in the literature of the world which has exactly the same quality. Oneness, unity, synthesis and identification exist today as words related to consciousness and as expressing what is at present unattainable to the mass of men. This manifesto or declaration of the Christ constitutes the first attempt to convey reaction to contact with Shamballa.[46]

A true meditative reflection on this keynote, leading to some measure of identification with it, can literally work wonders. A clear example of this on the world stage and within the religious field is the summons of Pope John XXIII to the Second Vatican Council. The passage, "that they may be one . . .", from John:17, was reportedly a favourite inspiration to His Holiness. The growth of general understanding in relation to planetary ecology and the interaction of the various kingdoms in nature gives us an inkling of what D.K. is trying to explain about the different 'centres' receiving energy within the organic and spiritual wholeness of planetary life. It validates in an all-inclusive way the hylozoistic basis of the secret doctrine which we considered in Chapter 1.

Many people are now conversant with the idea of energy centres existing within the subtle parts of the human make-up, and the possibility that these correspond to the human endocrine system (see Appendix C). If we can transfer this concept to the larger world picture, A.A.B.'s diagram (in Appendix A) may make additional sense.

I do realize that people sometimes have difficulty thinking in terms of correspondences; it is a way of coming to an understanding through a kind of analogy, and this is not always very satisfactory to the literal mind. I remember once looking down from a stair balcony onto a dance floor full of couples engaged in an old-fashioned waltz, spinning, turning, travelling, sometimes bumping into each other, and, apart from the variety of attraction in the ladies' evening dresses, I was suddenly reminded of a science film showing amoeba-like phenomena gyrating in fluid. The young lady beside me was deeply shocked at this unromantic vision, and I was strongly reprimanded for my unfortunate imagery.

Enough of all that; the major centres given throughout the teachings, in relation to the planetary life, are Shamballa representing the head, Hierarchy enshrining the heart centre, and mankind, representing the throat, as active intelligence.[47] D.K. explains:

There was a time when (in the early history of the planet) there was no Hierarchy; there were only two major centres in the expression of the life of the Lord of the World: Shamballa and His embryonic throat centre, Humanity. Shamballa was the head centre. There was no humanity, such as we now know it, but only something so primitive that it is well-nigh impossible for you to grasp its significance or factual expression. But the life of God was there, plus an inherent 'urge' and a dynamic 'pull'. These two factors rendered the mass of men (if one may call them so) inchoately invocative, thus drawing from high spiritual centres certain developed and informed Lives Who — in increasing numbers — 'walked among men' and led them slowly, very slowly, forward into increasing light. The early history of the Hierarchy falls into two historical eras in the process of its becoming a 'meditating Centre':

First: The time when the relating, mediating, enlightening correspondence to Those we now call the Masters trod the earth with men and were not withdrawn and apparently invisible, as is now the case. Their task was to bring the primitive intelligence of humanity to the point where there could be the presentation of the Plan, with eventual cooperation . . .

Second: The time when the Hierarchy was created as we know it today; the heart centre of Sanat Kumara came into its own life, formed its own magnetic field, possessed its own ring-pass-not, and became a dynamic mediating centre between Shamballa and Humanity.

It has oft been told in occult and theosophical literature that the Hierarchy withdrew as a penalising measure because of the wickedness of mankind. This is only superficially true and is an instance of a man-made interpretation, giving us the first example of the fear-and-punishment psychology which — from that time on — has conditioned all religious teaching. The withdrawing Masters had Their Paul to distort the truth, just as had the Christ, Their august Head today. The truth was far otherwise. [48]

Of course, at various times, the energy emanating through one or other planetary centre may flow into and through others. [49] What we might call the inhabiting lives can move in their development from one centre to another; in one early stage, humanity reportedly expressed the planetary solar plexus. Instances of this are discussed in the context of other subjects, but in order to try and keep a complex subject as simple as may be possible we will try to hold to the thread of the main theme. Do not, however, adopt any imagery too rigidly; simply encourage an exploratory attitude.

We are dealing with a vast, many-levelled growth movement, energetic, fluid and kaleidoscopic in the changing of its patterns throughout time. The ancient Chinese system of guidance, the *I Ching*, was rightly called 'the Book of Changes'. In a major tabulation for the future [50] we find a listing that gives Shamballa as head, the Hierarchy as heart, Humanity as *ajna* or 'third eye', animals as throat, vegetables as solar plexus, the devas as sacral centre and the mineral kingdom as base of the spine root centre. We can therefore follow indications [51] that there is anticipated in the course of immediate evolutionary development a particular flow of energy from the throat to the *ajna* or brow centre, in which mankind is vitally involved.

At a more tangible level, D.K. sites the five continents of earth [52] and claims: 'These five continents are to the planetary Life what five major endocrine glands are to the human being. They are related to five centres.' He also gives a considerable amount of information about what he calls 'spiritual inlets' [53] listing five cities in relation to various areas of the globe, corresponding them to centres within the human vehicle. [54] The five listed as active, at least to some degree, at the moment are London, New York, Geneva, Tokyo and Darjeeling. We learn that the cities came about because of the centres, not the other way round, though let us suppose the concentrations of humanity at these points must have some effect. Perhaps for practical purposes we could think of them to some extent as Bo-points upon the complex of humanity's energy meridians. (Bo-points are those acupuncture locations of especial value in stimulating energy flow.) In relation to other spiritual energy levels the centres can act, as is ever the case, as service gates.

Depending on the stance taken in time to individual kingdoms, the relationship and function can change; for example, in connection with humanity, the Hierarchy can function as the head centre. As with many of the subjects D.K. and A.A.B. have tried to open up, it is exceedingly hard to try and put all the detail into the proverbial nutshell without misrepresentation. On this occasion we can only encourage a new way of looking at the environment.

As indicated above, some aspects of planetary life await development. Where the spiritual potential of humanity is concerned, the position is recorded rather differently. [55] Certain factors are crucial, and hints given in connection to them are of immediate relevance:

The form of humanity is completed. Its right placement within the womb of matter is the objective of the Hierarchy, with all the consequent implications. Note these words. The need at this time is terrific, and the soul is at the birthing in humanity as a whole. Cosmically speaking, if right direction of the forces of the human kingdom is now achieved, there will be manifested on the earth a humanity which will manifest a purpose, a beauty and a form which will be full expressions of an inner spiritual reality and in line with (soul) purpose. Other eventualities can be sensed as sadly possible but these we will not consider for it is the hope and the belief of the watching Brothers that men will transcend all undesirable eventualities and make the goal. One word here, and one hint. The Hierarchy of the planet constitutes symbolically the head centre of humanity and their forces constitute the brain forces. On the physical plane are a large band of aspirants, probationary disciples and accepted disciples who are seeking to be responsive to the 'head centre', some consciously, others unconsciously. They are gathered from all fields of expression but are all creative in some way or other. They in their turn constitute what might be symbolically called the 'pineal gland' of humanity. As in individual man this is usually dormant or asleep, so, in humanity, this group of cells within the brain of the body corporate is dormant, but thrilling to the vibrations of the head centre — the occult Hierarchy. Some of the cells are awake. Let them intensify their endeavour and so awaken others. The pioneers of the human family, the scientists, thinkers and artists constitute the pituitary body. They express the concrete mind but lack that intuitive perception and idealism which would place them (symbolically speaking) in the pineal gland; they are nevertheless brilliant, expressive and investigating. The objective of the Hierarchy (again symbolically speaking) is to make the pineal gland so potent and, therefore, so attractive that the pituitary body of cell lives may be stimulated and thus a close interplay be brought about. This will lead to such potent action that there will be a streaming forth of new cells to the pineal gland and at the same time such a strong reaction set up that the entire body will be affected, resulting in the streaming upward of many stimulated lives to take the places of those who are finding their way into the centre of hierarchical endeavour. [56]

If we hark back to the extract offered in Chapter 1 on Sutra 32 of the yoga teaching of Patanjali (see page 30), we recall that the Charles Johnston version gave an imagery of 'that better and wiser consciousness behind the outward looking consciousness in the forward part of the head; that better and wiser consciousness "at the back of the mind" '. It is the relationship between the two that now concerns us. There is a great deal of research [57] nowadays into the need for interplay between the right and left hemispheres of the brain. There is also, I believe, a need for good communications between the boardroom and the front office, the fore and aft of human consciousness. D.K. puts it in another way:

We must note that a conscious relation has been established between the soul and its shadow, the man on the physical plane. *Both have been meditating.* Students would do well to note this and to remember that one of the objectives of the daily meditation is to enable the brain and mind to vibrate in unison with the soul as it seeks 'in meditation deep' to communicate with its reflection.

The correspondence to this relation or synchronizing vibration is interesting:

Soul	Man on the Physical Plane
Mind	Brain
Pineal Gland	Pituitary Body

It is also symbolized for us in the relation between the Eastern and Western hemispheres and between those great bodies of truth which we call Religion and Science. [58]

As for the individual so, in some measure, can it be for the group. And the above remarks could apply to the inner and outer seed-groups for specialized fields of service, which we have discussed. I would suggest that in the New Group of World Servers we have — symbolically speaking, as D.K. reiterates — an aspect of the pineal gland for the human race; but in a still larger sense, the Group is the vanguard of humanity's transfer into functioning activity as the *ajna* centre of the world, channelling, fusing and synthesizing energy from head, heart and throat centres, thus visioning and projecting the detail of the work, from cycle to cycle, for which our world came to birth.

So we will have, to use D.K.'s phrase, 'the focused attention of the soul in contemplation, acting through the head centre, focused in the region of the third eye and swept into right activity by an act of will'.[59] The five-pointed star of ascension (for the energy of solar plexus and sacral centre are also involved) can shine upon the brow and the combined energies be used in creative service;[60] only it will not be an achievement merely of one or two remarkable men and women here and there but a steady shining forth throughout the human race. In a book quoted earlier we find another hint:

The masonic tradition has the teaching clearly held in its beautiful ritual of the raising of the great Master Mason. Only when there is united effort of a five-fold kind, and only after repeated failure, does the vivifying life course through the entire body and bring to life the true man.

This interplay in the activity of the two major head 'glands' is the outcome of age-long growth and loving effort. Clear motive and work achieved combine to make it possible. No artificial aid or technical exercise will ultimately tempt the soul to inhabit its vehicle, however helpful such exercises may prove to be in disciplining the human body and preparing the ground. The centres have been termed 'gateways to service' awakened through growth in maturity,[61] but service itself is the response of a caring heart and intelligent goodwill. The fire of the human heart sparks off the dynamo. Prior to that, delays and obstacles stand guard, and it is our own safety that they protect.[62]

However, having said that and remembering how we commenced our study with a consideration of the science of impression, the following passage seems relevant in reaffirming what we have been considering:

It is therefore largely a matter of perfecting the mechanism of the brain so that it can rightly register and correctly transmit the soul impressions and the group purposes and recognitions. This involves:
1. The awakening into conscious activity of the centre between the eyebrows, called by the oriental student, the ajna centre.
2. The subordinating then of the activity of this centre to that of the head centre, so that the two vibrate in unison. This produces the establishment of three things:
    a) Direct conscious alignment between soul-mind-brain.
    b) The appearance of a magnetic field which embraces both the head centres and so definitely affects the pineal gland and the pituitary body.
    c) The recognition of this field of dual activity in two ways: as of a light in the head, an interior radiant sun, or as a dynamic centre of energy through which the will or purpose aspect of the soul can make itself felt. [63]

What can occur in the individual and be communicated to the multitude can demonstrate itself also in the collective and go round the world. Thus in a group sense the new world can, by means of this combined activity of the within and the without, which has been noted by many mystics, [64] be visualized and precipitated. In order to give a practical example and anchor our research firmly in the everyday of human life, let us look at a statement about such visualization made by Nikola Tesla, the prodigal and prodigious genius and inventor who has been called the man who invented in the twentieth century. It is interesting, in view of what D.K. wrote about the emergence of modern machines (page 100) that Tesla's biographer, John J. O'Neill, wrote:

He dedicated his life to bringing the burdens from the shoulders of mankind; to bringing a new era of peace, plenty and happiness to the human race . . . The inventions that this scientific martyr produced were designed for the peace, happiness and security of the human race, but they have been applied to create scarcity, depressions and devastating war . . . the experiment will have to be made many times more before we learn how to create a super race with the minds of Teslas that can tap the hidden treasure of Nature's store of knowledge, yet endowed too with the vital power of love that will unlock forces, more powerful than any which we now glimpse, for advancing the status of the human race. [65]

Tesla himself wrote in later life:

By that faculty of *visualizing*, which I learned in my boyish efforts to rid myself of annoying images, I have evolved what is, I believe, a new method of materializing inventive ideas and conceptions. It is a method which may be of great usefulness to any imaginative man, whether he is an inventor, businessman or artist.

Some people, the moment they have a device to construct or any piece of work to perform, rush at it without adequate preparation, and immediately become engrossed in details, instead of the central idea. They may get results, but they sacrifice quality.

Here, in brief, is my own method: After experiencing a desire to invent a particular thing, I may go on for months or years with the idea in the back of my head. Whenever I feel like it, I roam around in my imagination and think about the problem without any deliberate concentration. This is a period of incubation.

Then follows a period of direct effort. I choose carefully the possible solutions of the problem I am considering, and gradually center my mind on a narrowed field of investigation. Now, when I am deliberately thinking of the problem in its specific features, I may begin to feel that I am going to get the solution. And the wonderful thing is, that if I do feel this way, *then I know I have really solved the problem and shall get what I am after.*

The feeling is as convincing to me as though I already had solved it. I have come to the conclusion that at this stage the actual solution is in my mind *subconsciously*, though it may be a long time before I am aware of it *consciously*.

Before I put a sketch on paper, the whole idea is worked out mentally. In my mind I change the construction, make improvements, and even operate the device. Without ever having drawn a sketch I can give the measurements of all parts to workmen, and when completed all these parts will fit, just as certainly as though I had made the actual drawings. It is immaterial to me whether I run my machine in my mind or test it in my shop.

The inventions I have conceived in this way have always worked. In thirty years there has not been a single exception. My first electric motor, the vacuum tube wireless light, my turbine engine and many other devices have all been developed in exactly this way.[66]

Tesla seems to have employed the back and the front of the mind as well as a dynamic 'as if' technique. He had some peculiar ideas about the capacities inherent in vision, and some of his thinking in this respect (which Mr O'Neill feels could be mistaken) might possibly bear comparison with D.K.'s claims that etheric vision is a capacity of the physical eye rather than an interned subjectivity as he says is the case in astral clairvoyance. Some of Castanenda's remarks in this respect may also be pertinent.[67] The Secret Doctrine states: 'The opened or third eye does not convey direct clairvoyance, but is the organ through which direct and certain knowledge is obtained.'[68] However, this last statement also relates to its synthesizing capacity to assemble knowledge from several directions.

It is perhaps intriguing that in discussing training for the future and the inner development of would-be group workers, D.K. remarks: 'The clue to all this esoteric work demanded by Shamballa is to be found in the development of the Art of Visualization.'[69] The usual short shopping list of provisos and objectives follows this comment; however, these open several other cans of beans which we do not have time to pursue at the moment.

One of the Baileys' fairly early efforts in the context of the goodwill work was to launch a newspaper that would highlight news that was at least indicative of New Group-type stirrings.[70] They called it *The World Observer*, hoping, maybe, that it would visualize what could be achieved. But perhaps it was before its time, even if its appearance was not before it was needed; finance was lacking, the network of men and women of goodwill round the world was insufficiently in touch to prove responsive enough, and there was a world war en route to be lived through. Now the challenge seems to have been picked up by many magazines and journals. Some are properly house organs for worthy societies, while others follow specialized lines of work such as environmental interests, alternative energy, health care, education or what have you; there are also those which try to rove freely over a wide range of interest. Perhaps in their sum total they represent the newspaper of the men and women of goodwill, who visualize the explosive forces of the human scene transformed into a new world order.

In fact, the whole of the more than one hundred pages of Chapter Three of the second volume of *A Treatise on the Seven Rays* is devoted to a discussion of the New Group in relation to possible activities of people of goodwill, though necessarily this material is focused to tune in with the conditions existing at the time the passage was written. Elsewhere D.K. offered a simple prayer for those who wished to align their interior work with the New Group. It became known as 'the five o'clock prayer' because of what is written in the instruction accompanying it. Most people, I believe, consider it to be five o'clock in the afternoon — but why feel restricted if you happen to get up early? In any event it is always five o'clock somewhere around the globe, and this sort of suggestion, to my mind, simply stressed the fact that it is a continuous prayer:

It would be of value if each student would link up every day at five o'clock by an act of will with this rapidly integrating group of servers, mystics and brothers. To this end it might be wise to commit to memory the following brief dedication to be said silently at that hour with the attention focused in the head:

May the Power of the One Life pour through the group of all true servers.

May the Love of the One Soul characterize the lives of all who seek to aid the Great Ones.

May I fulfill my part in the One Work through self-forgetfulness, harmlessness and right speech.

Then carry the thought forward from the rapidly forming group of world-servers to the Great Ones who stand back of our world evolution.

This can be done in a few seconds of time wherever one may be and in whatever company, and will not only aid in the magical work of the forces of light, but will serve to stabilize the individual, to increase his group consciousness, and to teach him the process of carrying forward interior subjective activities in the face of and in spite of outer exoteric functioning. [71]

An emblem of visual symbols which was among the effects of Foster Bailey. Using this picture to integrate some of the themes we have dealt with in this book, we can observe in the overhanging triangle, the radiant 'Eye of God'; it could also be visualized as the protecting eye of Horus, or the directing eye of the New Group of world servers — the Ajna centre of the world.

Below is the compass, a symbol of the divine plan, like the shafts of directing light, projecting from the hand of the Ancient of Days (in William Blake's famous picture). The compass works in conjunction with the sextant (one-sixth of a circle) which determines right relations between objects, and in its resemblance to the face of a clock could be read as the measurement of an allotted span of time for the work undertaken.

In the centre of this active work on the plan is the sun, standing for the heart of the solar Logos, and radiating outwards through an eight-fold nimbus, like the King through the eight kingdoms of Shamballa.

Around this is the crescent of growing things, a greater sextant or chalice of the world, composed of grapes (wine — blood — life) and ears of corn (bread — body — economic satisfaction), and the palm

6. The Little Daughter of a Long-lost Son ¹

The Soul and Its Mechanism is one of A.A.B.'s own books, in which she dealt in a fairly straightforward way with the whole Eastern concept of energy chakras and the corresponding endocrine glandular system, still under research by science. However, to use this scheme of things, albeit symbolically in the first instance, to interpret the potential function of human groups, is, I appreciate, a lot to ask people to digest. To consider human beings in groups as though they were highly individualistic atoms within cell-like structures, and this without any loss of human quality, is something I would not embark on if it did not seem to be important. D.K. appears adamant in his wish to see right relations prevail between the esoteric sphere of living energies and the mechanisms through which they can manifest:

At this point I would remind you that *the effect of the impact of energy is dependent upon the nature of the vehicle of response.* According to his equipment and the nature of his bodies, so will man react to the inflowing energies. This is a fundamental statement. It is a law and

---

or mimosa (as seen, for example, in the hands of the populace outside the temple in Mozart's 'The Magic Flute', or before Christ's entry into Jerusalem), both of which are plants depicting the sun.

Of course each symbol can be read in a variety of ways, and with amplified meaning at different levels. In some mystery teachings, for instance, the wine or grape, which can be read as the vitality of life, can also in another context represent intoxication, either inspirational or diversionary. In our context we could be aware of the bunch of grapes as the autonomous seed-groups, each one connected to the one vine, yet complete in its own way and carrying seed.

The whole picture is emblematic of life-enhancing solar and spiritual influence, spreading or radiating from the centre to the periphery.

should be most carefully considered . . . The use each makes of the stimulating energy will be different; the focus of his consciousness is very different; his type of mind is quite different; his centres, their activity and their internal organization are different. And it is the same for groups, organizations and nations.

Nations, for instance, have seven centres, as have all forms of existence from the human and animal upwards, and it is an interesting study to discover these centres and note the type of energy which flows through them . . . This information constitutes one of the major hierarchical sciences and indicates to us who know it the possibilities latent in any nation, the point of attainment and the opportunities for work and advancement, or the obstacles to progress; this is gauged by the light in the centres and the heightening and the obscuration of their vibration. It is this that makes possible or hinders the growth of what is called spirituality in individuals and in nations, and this science will later be recognized. It is by means of this science that the Hierarchy can form its larger plans and know in what manner individual nations will react to stimulation and to progress of the desired kind. [2]

The 'third eye' focus of energy, when it is to some extent integrated and developing in a human being, group or national life, can demonstrate the 'straight-knowledge of the heart'. In other words, it is a channel for understanding born of empathy and intuition. It sees behind appearances and beyond events. It is the ascendant star upon the brow, whose agency synthesizes the energy of the other centres. As it functions creatively to visualize the good, the true and the beautiful, it also helps set in motion those forces that bring them into practical manifestation. The New Group of World Servers, in so far as that subjective grouping manages to act as the *ajna* centre of the world, is therefore an agency for creating a more beneficent future. [3]

In a recent book, *The Metamorphic Technique*, Gaston Saint-Pierre and Debbie Boater discuss a growth practice where the practitioner, using massage techniques similar though not exactly the same as those employed in Reflexology, aims to act as an impersonal catalyst in order to release the individual's energy patterns from blockage. Practitioners are, in so far as this can be understood, not simply seeking a cure for isolated and possibly superficial outer conditions but are attempting to open out a way whereby the 'timeless' element in the human being can operate in relation to the earthly vehicle. (Another form of Browning's 'opening out a way whence the imprisoned splendour may escape'). Quoting an article on the work of the Nobel prize-winning doctors Roger Guillemin and Andrew Schally, whose work included study of the pituitary body, and Dr Karl König's *Meditations on the Endocrine Glands*, they suggest:

that the pineal gland is the entry point of consciousness, the highest point of knowledge within us, yet almost dormant in modern man. It is interesting to note that above this gland is found the fontanelle, which remains open in us until well after birth. Below the pineal comes the pituitary, known as the 'master gland' of the endocrine system as it directly influences all the other glands. Here it would appear that the higher knowledge of the pineal is being channelled onto earth through the pituitary.[4]

— all of which seems to march in response and in resonance with what we have just been discovering via A.A.B.'s D.K. scripts.

Amongst the very many aids for the development of consciousness which D.K. included in his teaching work are six Formulas of Revelation, which he maintained had applications for the future. Information about them is interspersed throughout a nearly 200-page section of 'Teachings on Initiation' in one of A.A.B.'s books.[5] Were we able, he reports, to enter the archives where these instructions are held we would discover

Six large sheets of some unknown metal. These look as if made of silver and are in reality composed of that metal which is the allotrope of silver and which is therefore to silver what the diamond is to carbon. Upon these sheets are words, symbols and symbolic forms. These, when related to each other, contain the formulas which the disciple has to interpret and integrate into his waking consciousness. This must be done through the medium of living processes.[6]

The formulas often seem at first glance to relate to well-known symbols but later appear more comprehensive and more complex: any study of them leaves one, as does a Zen puzzle, with a strong sense of a lot more waiting to be discovered. One brief example is of a square containing a circle with radiating lines, bounded by phrases or approximate translations thereof: 'Fiery Relations', 'Airy Expansion', 'Earthy Contact' and 'Oceanic Synthesis'. In one rendering he gives it as overleaf:

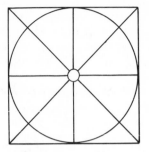

and quotes without reference:

All paths meet at the centre. The many become the seven and the eight.
From point to point the lines converge. They stretch from point to point.
The outer square, the circle of the One and the point of unity are seen
as one, and the Master passes on His way.[7]

It relates, we are told, to the construction of the group
antahkarana or bridge through mind to spirit. One cannot help
being reminded of the mandala of Shamballa, with its eight
regions and central citadel. D.K. tries to make it easier to
understand by likening the formula to a flag representing a
people's aspiration: 'They (flags) have of course been prostituted
to signify national separativeness and selfishness and national
patriotism, but behind the flag is a point of inspiration to the
soul of the people'.[8] Looking at this little diagram it is not
impossible to visualize the flag of the United Nations with the
globe of our world at its centre, and to see this in the light of
the formula.

Material on rules and suggestions for group progress is to be
found in many of the books, including nearly 300 pages on
'Fourteen Rules for Group Initiation'.[9] And some of the books
seem to offer themselves as textbooks for individual organons
or seed-groups, at least from the point of view of esoteric work.[10]
I do not think anyone attempting sensible, objective work would
wish to confine themselves to a diet of A.A.B.'s instructions; nor
is that the School's intention when getting the interested student
to open up his interior aspiration by thinking in terms of outgoing
service action — the job is one of making constructive
relationships. However, more than enough material is there in
the A.A.B. literature to kick the triggers and make a start. If we
are at all interested in this type of approach to life we need to

discover whether we are up to discovering fresh cultural roots more firmly embedded in the principles of the ageless wisdom than our frequently superficial international society now allows.

Perhaps we should not leave this subject of invoking future possibilities, and of discovering the part that seed-groups can play in being custodial doorkeepers to the great Museum of Future Potential which exists within the auric radiation of the great Household, without mentioning the counterpart of the New Group which exists at a still deeper level. In the diagram given in Appendix A, D.K. shows the divine Contemplatives or Nirmanakayas who act as links between the Lodge on High and the Father's House. ('Those perfected beings who renounce Nirvana and choose a life of self-sacrifice, becoming members of that invisible host which ever protects humanity within karmic limits.'[11])

Throughout his thirty-year mission D.K. emphasizes the importance of the interrelatedness of those primary kingdoms in nature, Shamballa, Hierarchy and Humanity, and consequently of the agents mediating between them. In 1946,[12] after the close of world hostilities and before the annual Wesak ceremony where the theosophic tradition maintains the Buddha brings the blessing of Shamballa to the assembled Lodge, D.K. spoke most briefly of the formation of a new ashram within the Household, which is concerned with the endowments of wisdom necessary for applying the will-to-good of the Shamballa force. However one may feel personally about this type of pronouncement, one of the points he seems to be trying to get across is that this particular channel for energetic wisdom is governed by an emblematic triangle composed of the Buddha, the Christ and the Lord of Civilization, representing in themselves the three great kingdoms already united in action. On this source of functional energy the New Group, and through them the men and women of goodwill, can draw. Whether any group or individual cares to see the potentially unified interplay of the three great kingdoms in this guise is probably of little real importance so long as they can feel the reality of the sustaining vitality within the shrine of their own souls.

Perhaps I go too far in this attempt to penetrate the type of planetary activity, subliminal to us, which A.A.B. maintained was taking place within the world which we also inhabit. So often it is some tiny event within personal life that will help an individual to register the reality of some quite profound and far-reaching concept. But until that happening, whatever it may be, has taken place, the concept in question is barely grounds for hypothesis. I remember once being invited to visit a lady who, in terms of outward activity, represented a large international corporation founded as the result of an inventive process — almost a household name — which her husband had produced. The work, however, that concerned her at heart was achieved in meditation, and this form of activity had been for her a lifelong occupation. I visited her in a private penthouse suite in a famous hotel, and the years of meditative work she had undertaken surrounded her like an almost tangible atmosphere. Within such a climate of understanding the idea of a Nirmanakaya meditating the divine plan into existence seemed more real. I do not mean that this lady, anchoring herself and her aides with a sustaining lunch in her private dining-room, was a Nirmanakaya (this would belie the meaning of the name of this Buddhic entity, which suggests[13] that it is without a body as we know it) but simply that both the presence she engendered and what she represented in her life provided a window onto realities other than those in which we customarily walk.

Incidentally, in *The Voice of the Silence*, transmitted by Madame Blavatsky,[14] we read that Gautama Buddha and some of his Arhats are such Nirmanakayas 'higher than whom, on account of the great renunciation and sacrifice to mankind there is none known'. D.K. refers to this[15] when he discusses a certain type of advanced Monad capable of a triple, simultaneous manifestation, showing forth as 'a Master in the three worlds, as a Bodhisattva on his own plane and as the emancipated Dhyani Buddha, yet these three will be but one'. But he continues later, after discussing the implications: 'As yet, there are not many progressed enough to do this triple work; the Buddha and nine others being the only Ones as yet remaining in touch with our particular planet in this particular manner.' A supreme enneagrammatic pattern-group, if you like.

Enough of that. Nancy Magor once told me a story of an admirer who invited her out to lunch. The young man had for some reason been on the edge of a desert in Africa. There, in a hut, he had found the fragmented remains of a book which he felt would be her cup of tea. Unfortunately, this tender present had been badly eaten by white ants. The book in question was

First Principles of Theosophy by Jinarajadasa. She was just able to decipher the address of the London headquarters of the Theosophical Society on a tattered fly leaf. She made contact with the Society and found a lifetime's work; while the courier, I believe, passed out of her life. It seems to me, as I try to pack a few more items into the remaining pages, that my function here has been extremely white ant-like: I have nibbled away and provided only a fraction of the material on which some of A.A.B.'s work was based. That which is given I have tried to present in a reasonably understandable structure. It is not more than a portion of A.A.B.'s total work and it is certainly not a presentable précis of D.K.'s teaching, but hopefully a sense of direction can be discovered in some of these pages. This will leave people free to press on with their own journey in their own way, while making what use they will of the signposts that they can distinguish.

White ant-like, we should observe that D.K. foretells that:

This group now in process of forming, will in time, develop its own 'yoga' and school of training which will gradually supersede that of the raja yoga and the bhakti yoga schools . . . The keynote of the new yoga will be synthesis; its objective will be conscious development of the intuitive faculty. This development will fall into two categories: first, the development of the intuition and of true spiritual perception, and secondly, the trained utilization of the mind as an interpreting agent. [16]

This last remark seems to apply to the dual pineal/pituitary relationship we have noted, which, while it happens symbolically between the representative groups we have discussed, can also take place in the course of individual expansion of consciousness.

Of course, right at the very beginning of the transcriptions taken by A.A.B. [17] there was a short, straightforward mention of the One fundamental school of life development rooted in Shamballa. This apparently maintains four branches in terms of manifestation, [18] the so-called trans-Himalayan branch being that with which many of the theosophical teachings, including A.A.B.'s writings, concern themselves. One as yet outwardly unestablished branch is of some interest in relation to the type of work discussed in this book. The references to it are fleeting but crop up in several places, [19] along with an invitation to ponder the significance of the imparted facts. The earliest reference is

simple and straightforward: 'The Master R. and one of the English
Masters are concerning themselves with the gradual founding
of the fourth branch of the school, with the assistance of the
Master Hilarion.' This tells the general reader very little, but in
a later publication we learn in a discussion on the seventh ray
(of ceremonial order and magic, a poetic title that conceals as
much as it reveals), that:

The seventh ray influence is that which will produce in a peculiar and
unexpected sense the Western school of occultism just as the sixth ray
(of idealism — JRS) impulse has produced the Eastern school of
occultism — the latter bringing the light down to the astral plane and
the new incoming influence carrying it down to the physical . . . The
roles will eventually be reversed and the shift of the 'light in the East'
will be over Europe and America. This will inevitably bring about the
needed and desired synthesis of the mystical way and the occult path.

In simple words, where before great spiritual and poetic scriptures
enshrined the vision and evoked the aspiration of the devotee,
now down-to-earth human welfare, backed by practical goodwill,
is the order of the day.

Certainly, as far as the remnants of strictly Tibetan tantric
philosophy and mystical Buddhism are concerned, circumstances
in Tibet have now contrived to have the teaching brought into
the European and American environments. This in itself must
produce a fertile cultural exchange, quite apart from any more
subliminal influence. Europe has, of course, during the last few
centuries been weaving its own Hermetic tradition, [20] seeded from
older schools of philosophy. And in America, the modern
metaphysical movement, also anciently rooted, [21] makes a most
interesting contribution. It is intriguing to look back at the work
of Emma Curtis Hopkins, who is sometimes considered a student
of Mary Baker Eddy, the founder of Christian Science, but was,
I am told, [22] a fellow student in Quimby's original class. Her
approach through the High Watch Fellowship and as a teacher
of other teachers has the same eclectic quality as the writings of
her more or less contemporary, though forerunner by a few years,
Madame Blavatsky. There is a universality in their source material
which gives a world perspective to what they are trying to impart,
and this consequently sparks other enterprises.

This, I believe, is a most important factor. Regardless of the regional influence or anchorage in any aspect, department or what you care to call it, of the One fundamental school, it is world work with which all mainstreams of teaching are concerned. The New Group is that network of subjective linkage between world workers with a planetary outlook: an outlook that concerns itself with all peoples and the life ecology of one united earth. This stance was paramount to the Baileys' outlook. D.K. acknowledged Mrs Besant's efforts as a world worker,[23] and it is interesting that Rukmini Devi, widow of a former theosophical president and founder of the Kalakshetra (Abode of Art), should have been considered by some to be a suitable nominee for the office of President of India.[24] Although she declined the honour, and regardless of other factors involved, the quality of her work and the scope of her outlook must have gained the attention of those of her countrymen willing to promote her. Joel Goldsmith, a modern metaphysical teacher, always held out the goal of world work behind any form of spiritual development.[25] The essential law of compassion[26] alone can provide the bonding which will facilitate those who want to join their efforts to those of 'The Hearts of Fiery Love', as members of the hierarchical Lodge have been called.

As far as aspirants are concerned the one thing the Masters are endeavouring to bring about is *the stimulation of the flame of the Spirit in them* so that they may set the world on fire. The fires of judgement and of substance, of karma and its vehicle matter, are raging in the world at this time. Fire must be countered by fire as well you know and to stop the inferno which is devastating the world, the fire of the spirit must be distributed and effectively used by the disciples of the Masters. The fire which must be used in the final analysis, by the disciples in the world, is the fire of the will to love.[27]

The subject of fire in its three esoteric aspects, fire by friction, solar fire and cosmic fire which goes into the whole hylozoistic concept of energy is the subject of an extremely detailed book, *A Treatise on Cosmic Fire.* Perhaps it is this volume of A.A.B.'s that most closely approaches Madame Blavatsky's *Secret Doctrine* material and indeed claims to be a psychological companion to that work.

As an aspect of fire, there are several hints in this work about the energy within the atom; and elsewhere, D.K. made a definite prophecy concerning the release of atomic energy:

It might be noted here that three great discoveries are imminent and during the next two generations will revolutionize modern thought and life.

One is already sensed and is the subject of experiment and investigation, the releasing of the energy of the atom. This will completely change the economic and political situation in the world, for the latter is largely dependent upon the former. Our mechanical civilization will be simplified, and an era ushered in which will be free from the incubus of money (its possession and its non-possession), and the human family will recognize universally its status as a bridging kingdom between the three lower kingdoms of nature and the fifth or spiritual kingdom. There will be time and freedom for a soul culture which will supersede our modern methods of education, and the significance of soul powers and the development of the super-human consciousness will engross the attention of educators and students everywhere. [28]

This statement was written in the early 1930s and was followed by another which was sent out from the Lucis Trust office in New York, date-stamped 5 August 1945, just after the announcement in the press of the explosion of the first atomic bomb. This statement has been printed in *The Externalization of the Hierarchy*, more or less as issued them:

I would like at this time to touch upon the greatest spiritual event which has taken place upon our planet since the fourth kingdom in nature, the human kingdom, appeared. I refer to the release of atomic energy . . .

Man's attention is normally focused on the externalities of living. Nevertheless, all great discoveries, such as those made in connection with astronomy or in relation to the laws of nature or involving such a revelation as that of radio-activity or the epoch making event announced this week concerning the first steps taken in the harnessing of cosmic energy, are ever the result of inner pressure, emanating from Forces and Lives, found in high places. Such inner pressures themselves function under the laws of the Spirit and not just under what you call natural laws; they are the result of the impelling work of certain great Lives, working in connection with the third aspect of divinity, that of active intelligence and are concerned with the substance or matter aspect of manifestation. Such activities are motivated from Shamballa . . .

Eventually, disciples upon the physical levels of activity become aware of the inner ferment and this happens either consciously or unconsciously. They become 'impressed' and the scientific work is then started and carried through into the stages of experimentation and final success.

The release of the energy of the atom is as yet in an extremely embryonic stage; humanity little knows the extent or the nature of the energies which have been tapped and released. There are many types of atoms, constituting the 'world substance'; each can release its own type of force; this is one of the secrets which the new age will in time reveal but a good and sound beginning has been made. I would call your attention to the words 'the liberation of energy'. It is *liberation* which is the keynote of the new era, just as it has ever been the keynote of the spiritually oriented aspirant. This liberation has started by the release of an aspect of matter and the freeing of some of the soul force within the atom. This has been, for matter itself, a great and potent initiation, paralleling those initiations which liberate or release the souls of men. [29]

Obviously the full measure of D.K.'s early prophecy has not yet been fulfilled. In relation to the releasing effect that atomic energy could already have on humanity's life style and also on the economic and other ideas we discussed in Chapters 2 and 3 the influence of fear has quite clearly had a most debilitating effect.

The destructive aspect of atomic energy and its undoubted potential danger, magnified by our own inability to get on with our own species, has hypnotized the public. Fortunately, if D.K. is to be believed, the possibilities of research and discovery are not at an end. [30] The means so far discovered for the liberation of energy are not the only ones available. As far as control is concerned, the most disappointing aspect of the whole business must be man's inability to control himself, which consequently makes the wise channelling of those forces increasingly at his command, extremely hazardous. But for this we can hardly accuse the unfortunate atom of being at fault. As time proceeds, man will gradually do four things:

1. Recover past knowledge and powers developed in Atlantean days.
2. Produce bodies resistant to the fire elementals of the lower kind which work in the mineral kingdom.
3. Comprehend the inner meaning of radioactivity, or the setting loose of the power inherent in all elements and all atoms of chemistry, and in all true minerals.

4. Reduce the formulas of the coming chemists and scientists to, *sound*, and not simply formulate through experiment on paper. In this last statement lies (for those who can perceive) the most illuminating hint that it has been possible as yet to impart on this matter. [31]

In connection with the above statement, D.K.'s own given plans for some of his future work are not without interest; elsewhere in the same book, [32] he says he is 'planning to restore' via his students' some of the old and occult methods of healing and to demonstrate: a) the place of the etheric body, b) the effect of pranic force, c) the opening up of etheric vision.

As one might expect from someone allegedly interested in the laboratories of the world, with the great philanthropic world movements, such as the Red Cross, and with the rapidly developing welfare movements [33], the whole subject of health and healing receives a great deal of attention. It is mentioned in many of the books, but particularly in *A Treatise on the Seven Rays*, Vol. IV and in *A Treatise on Cosmic Fire*. However, the effect of a great deal of the material is to make evident the limited spectrum of man's actual knowledge and possibly to assist one in learning to hold one's soul in patience. Almost every aspect of the subject receives a mention, whether it is diet, exercise, medical preparations or specific diseases. The tenor of the information is in tune with much of what now comes under the wide-ranging domain of holistic medical care. But time and again, what is said is an allusion or hint on the way research might go; no patent cures or ready-made prescriptions are on offer.

Little public progress seems to have taken place in relation to research on the etheric or vital nature of man, although the results of Dr Harold Saxon Burr's investigation did raise interest. [34] However, laser beam techniques show that a whole branch of energy therapy is a practical potential, capable of the most delicate work; and the quiet, patient work of medics like Dr Shafica Karagulla, experienced in both neurology and psychiatry, into the subtle energy content of subjects with whom she has researched the field, helps to keep the quest alive. [35] Also, the renewed interest and research in the East as well as the West into such ancient therapies as acupuncture with its emphasis on the Ch'i energy could well qualify as the restoration of an old method of healing. Curiously enough, the special interest in such

techniques amongst Western nations, has, through the work of
Sidney Rose-Neil[36] and others, produced some response among
Third World countries who cannot handle the expense of a totally
modern allopathic health system for all their people and must
perforce consider blending the traditional ways with Western
science as well as with those alternative therapies that become
available. Others such as Professor Michio Kushi and his
colleagues[37] have done a great deal of educative work in making
the Eastern approach better understood by Western minds. I
choose these names as almost random examples of different lines
of work, and must again emphasize that it is not my intention
to tie these good people to the Bailey wagon just because they
cover some of the same territory.

There is more than enough work for a multitude of research
assistants to approach the common task from where they will.
Many groups[38] are assembling useful facts in the pursuit of cures
for such persistent scourges as cancer; others are processing
information on who is doing what. Behind the great quest for
the alleviation of suffering and the cure of disease abide the eternal
pursuit of the philosopher's stone and the strange, alchemical
dreams of youthful immortality that haunt the human race:

The sons of God, who know and see and hear (and knowing, know
they know) suffer the pain of conscious limitation. Deep in the inmost
depths of conscious being, their lost estate of liberty eats like a canker.
Pain, sickness, poverty and loss are seen as such, and from them every
son of God revolts. He knows that in himself, as once he was before
he entered prisoner into form, he knew not pain. Sickness and death,
corruption and disease, they touched him not. The riches of the universe
were his, and naught he knew of loss.[39]

So runs one of D.K.'s quotes from ancient records. The idea of
great lives, beyond our comprehension, affecting nature's tides
and turnings, as indicated in the passage about atomic energy,
may be hard to digest. Just as the concept of our little human
seed-groups acting like cellular focii within a vast comprehensive
living creature may be quite as difficult to swallow. Yet D.K.
went on from there to introduce the thought that beyond our
little world's cyclic life and far, far beyond our individual
manifestations upon the surface of the earth, other great paths
of life await the spirit graduating from this 'planet of painful

endeavour'. [40] It seems there is little one can usefully relate about the mass of material which he divulged on such cosmic centres as Sirius, which he terms a parent system to our own. [41] Except to mention the emphasis which he claims its radiation places on the theme of freedom as this affects what we call civilization, [42] thus influencing cause and inevitable effect and the ability of the resilient human spirit to extricate itself from totalitarian imposition, despite the seemingly dire cost at our level which this freeing of ourselves sometimes requires. Yet these, he would maintain, are the impressive influences within the liberating trend of which he wrote. And even though one can make little intelligent comment on such themes, I feel impelled to mention them in passing on, for they are an integral part of A.A.B.'s anchoring effort. In any case, I believe, such matters have a proper place within the emerging New Age myths whose subliminal current can carry us in good and healthy directions, especially so as we come to understand a little more about the trend of the tide.

Robert Temple embarked upon the seven or eight years of painstaking research which led to his book *The Sirius Mystery* without ever having heard of A.A.B., D.K. or his teaching; [43] only to those reading both could some items appear to coincide. No one instructed the public to rise to welcome the living myth when it came to them clothed so skilfully in Doris Lessing's inventive *Canopus in Argos: Archives* series of novels. Throughout we are dealing with matters which can be noted down on the pages of books and stories, but in fact have their true dwelling within the living consciousness of the people.

And if we say little about this, we have spoken not at all of a great portion of A.A.B.'s work. During the last three years of her life, as she strove to complete her assignment with D.K., taking his dictation when he could manage to give it [44] and doing what could be done to set up the future of her own work, she was centred more and more within the Mansion and beside the one who had given impulse to the whole work. [45] Foster Bailey wrote: [46]

Some have asked why she should have had to suffer — for she did suffer mentally and emotionally as well as physically. I alone know how triumphantly she opened herself to receive the impact of many types of destructive forces so rampant in this time of world turmoil and how amazingly she transmuted them, thus safeguarding all those hard pressed, struggling aspirants and younger disciples who have come to her, and to her School through the years.

By far the greater part of her life work has always been subjective. We have seen the outer effects, watched the outer comings and goings, helped her and loved her, sometimes criticized; sometimes complained, but always gone on, with her and because of her, yet a little higher and a little better than would otherwise have been the case. We are all very human and she was very human too.

Why did she suffer? Because her chosen path is on the line of the World Saviours.[46]

Again we might ask what this may mean, and whether perhaps it is the rhetoric of the wake? However, there is a service arising out of the practice of harmlessness which will make sense to many in the religious life, and mean something to those metaphysicians whose healing treatment sees energy impersonally and can nullify its toxic effects. Tibetan Buddhists sometimes practice emptiness, and when the 'hungry ghosts' surround them clamouring to be fed, they invite them joyously to fill themselves on all that space.

There is . . . a later stage wherein the disciple learns to absorb and transmute the wrong vibrations and the energies which are destructive. He has no shells nor barriers. He does not insulate himself nor isolate himself from his brothers. Through harmlessness he has learnt to neutralize all evil emanations. Now he acts with a positiveness of a new kind. Definitely and with full awareness of what he is doing, he gathers into himself all the evil emanations (destructive energies and wrong forces) and he breaks them up into their component parts and returns them whence they came, neutralized, impotent and harmless, yet intact in nature. You say that this is a hard teaching and conveys but little to the average aspirant? Such is ever the way in esoteric teaching, but those who know will understand and for them I speak.[47]

The whole subject of saviours, avatars, 'the Rider on the White Horse'[48] and messengers including the contentious matter of the reappearance of Christ, about which A.A.B. produced a whole book,[49] and which D.K. maintained could happen, like the liberation of atomic energy, in several different ways[50] — all this awaits the reader's investigation. And the subject has to be considered in the context of the even larger book which D.K. used to focus primarily on the imminent (in terms of the time scales with which he tends to deal) re-emergence of some members of the Lodge into the 'light of day'.[51] For D.K. would have us believe that some divine men are to reappear as a working group within external world affairs. However, throughout his presentation of this thought he offers no 'cargo cult', no diverting fireworks, no free passage from responsibility. Cavafy's famous poem about waiting for the barbarians is to the point here; we cannot, it seems, sit down and say 'Those people are some sort of solution,' the implication being quite literally that they will arrive with the solution, but not before it. Christ himself saw the psychological danger 2,000 years ago and warned that at the end of the age, people would say, 'Lo, here; lo, there'[52] Mrs Mary Bailey told a conference not long ago that she felt sure there would be no television interviews except in the line of workaday duty. D.K. was, for him, quite abrupt: 'They come with no herald, and only their works will proclaim them.'[53]

At the end of one of the early volumes[54] in the mighty *Treatise on the Seven Rays* (3,360 pages long without indexes), D.K. gave some objectives for the New Group of world servers which seem to have a particular application for anyone interested in A.A.B.'s work who might care to align themselves with the proffered horizon, the first being 'to discover, educate and blend together the men of goodwill'. This covers the study of human problems, the efforts for ecumenical and international understanding, the schemes for betterment in human relations and the creative attempts to educate public attitudes. Secondly there is the use of prayer and invocation in 'acts of appeal' to those forces of light available for human succour. This includes the rhythm of the full moon solar approaches. One of A.A.B.'s final public meetings in the UK was devoted to an explanation of the capacity that the Great Invocation, as it came to be called (see Appendix D), has for linking and relating the three main kingdoms on our planet: Light (humanity), Love (the hierarchical Lodge) and Power (the Father's House, Shamballa).[55] This increasingly conscious relationship between the three areas of planetary life, in terms of energy interchange, is indigenous to the subject matter of all A.A.B.'s work. D.K. once quoted a pictorial description from one of the ubiquitous archives:

The point of the triangle is based in the Courts of Heaven (Shamballa) and from that point two streams of power pour forth into the realm of soul and into the heart of the disciple. Thus is the Triad formed; then are the energies related unto the world of men; thus can the will of God appear, and thus can the Great Lord Who guards the Council Chamber of this sphere of solar Life carry His purpose to the holy groups (the ashrams — A.A.B.) and thence into the minds of men, and this because their hearts are safeguarded by the fire of love.[56]

This, he said, applies to the period immediately before us, of which the work he is trying to do is just a tiny living part. His third objective was:

To hold before humanity, as part of the living instruction which the men of goodwill will teach and live out in their daily lives, the necessity of a great group participation in a Day of Forgiveness and Forgetting.[57]

A day of invocation is held annually at the full moon of June by many groups; I do not know of a day of forgiveness. Some people make recollection at the other end of the spiritual year, and celebrate a day of alignment with the New Group on 21 December. Perhaps forgiveness could become a practice linked with that. But how to set about it when there is so much bitterness installed, so much hatred loose in the world and so much fear to pass through?

I do not know that I could forget; and I do not suppose others would find it any easier, even though we learn the lesson inevitably as we pass through the gates of death. Horror can make its own impression. Yet D.K.'s advice is basic to all metaphysics and central to much spiritual instruction. *High Mysticism* devotes a chapter to for-giveness: *A Course in Miracles* enshrines it as a tenet.[58] What we have understood of D.K.'s practice of harmlessness does the same. And here he advises that in the universality of human error, it is not a question of magnanimity, expediency or superiority, but 'a desire to forget the past, and to push forward into the new age, the new relationship and the new civilization.'[59] Elsewhere,[60] he pleaded: 'Let us drop our antagonisms and our antipathies, and think in terms of the one family, the one life and the one humanity.' In this respect we can only, in great quietness of spirit, practise the metaphysical rule and give the treatment to ourselves, knowing that holistically and hologrammatically the unit is reflective of the Whole Self in whom it lives and moves and has its being. If we can do that one simple thing — if we can forgive ourselves and experience some sense of release from our own imprisonment — then perhaps we shall be able to move forward once again to take another step upon the way: 'Father, forgive us, we know not what we do.'

The tale of the prodigal son is a cosmic story. D.K. reflects upon it[61] and relates Christ's parable to the Sons of God who refused to leave the Father's Home and make the sacrifice of incarnation, wishing ever to remain in their high place, as told in the legend of the 'war in heaven'. However, the version well known to us gives Christ's emphasis on the triumphal return: 'And he arose, and came to his father. But when he was yet a great way off, his father saw him, and had compassion, and ran, and fell on his neck, and kissed him.'[62] Symbolically, the neck speaks for the rainbow bridge that joins us to the directing care of our source. It is emblematic of the antahkarana. And the compassion of the great Household greets us on that homing way. How deep this ancient story goes we cannot say; that it may apply to our solar system or our Logos, as it does to the human race and to ourselves, is even possible. An ancient record speaks tenderly of our earth as 'the little daughter of a long lost son'.[63] We are told:

When light illuminates the minds of men and stirs the secret light within all forms, then the One in Whom we live reveals His hidden secret lighted Will.

When the purpose of the Lords of Karma can find no more to do, and all the weaving and close-related plans are all worked out, then the One in Whom we live can say: 'Well done! Naught but the beautiful remains.'

When the lowest of the low, the densest of the dense, and the highest of the high have all been lifted through the little wills of men, then can the One in Whom we live raise into radiating light the vivid lighted ball of Earth, and then another greater Voice can say to Him: 'Well done! Move on. Light shines!'[64]

Appendix A

The ongoing alignment between three major kingdoms in nature, which is now affecting the science of impression and spiritual contact:

This is but a rough picture and one which is not totally correct; it will, however, show you certain lines of contact and of relationship which *are* true and which will suffice to give you a vague and general idea of the new alignment being set up between the three major planetary centres.

I.   First Planetary Centre   .Shamballa
         [working through]
     1. The seven Rays or the seven Spirits before the Throne.
     2. Certain great Intermediaries.
     3. The Council Chamber of the Lord of the World.

II. Second Planetary Centre   .Hierarchy
         [working through]
     1. The seven major Chohans and Their Ashrams.
     2. The forty-nine Masters of the secondary Ashrams.
     3. The sum total of the secondary Ashrams.

III. Third Planetary Centre   .Humanity
         [working through]
     1. Disciples in manifestation — of the seven ray types.
     2. The new group of world servers.
     3. The sum total of humanitarians, educators and men of goodwill.

The Externalization of the Hierarchy,
'Stages in the Externalization', p.528.

The keynote of the Lord of the World is HUMANITY for it is the basis, the goal and the essential inner structure of all being. Humanity itself is the key to all evolutionary processes and to all correct understanding of the divine Plan, expressing in time and space the divine Purpose. Why He chose that this should be so, we know not; but it is a point to be accepted and remembered in all study of the Science of Impression because it is the factor that makes relationship and contact possible and it is also the source of all understanding.

Telepathy and the Etheric Vehicle, pages 126-7

From the human family, all divine Lives and Beings have come; in humanity the creative process is constantly working; and into humanity all sub-human lives must eventually proceed. As regards the meditative creative process, the diagram below may serve somewhat to clear your minds.

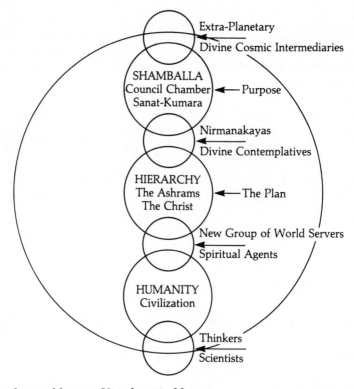

The three subhuman Kingdoms in Nature.
Esoterically, the reflection of the three major groups, listed above.
Discipleship in the New Age, Vol. II, p. 214.

Appendix B

The seven qualified ray energies referred to in I.1, Appendix A, have been charted as below. The names vary slightly in different accounts of their activity. We are, in the Western hemisphere, unaccustomed to personifying energies in this way; however, this does not invalidate the points made in the teaching.

THE SOLAR HIERARCHY
The Solar Logos.

|

The Solar Trinity or Logoi
I   The Father ....Will.
II   The Son ....Love-Wisdom.
III   The Holy Spirit ....Active Intelligence.

|

The Seven Rays
Three Rays of Aspect.
Four Rays of Attribute.
I Will or Power ...II Love-Wisdom ...III Active Intelligence

|

4. Harmony or Beauty.
5. Concrete Knowledge.
6. Devotion or Idealism.
7. Ceremonial Magic

Initiation, Human & Solar, page 49. *Treatise on Cosmic Fire*, page 1239.

The properties and function of each ray and the many ways, both macrocosmic and microcosmic, in which they manifest and interweave their energies are the subject of a huge dissertation published by A.A.B. in five volumes under the title *A Treatise on the Seven Rays.* The most concise description I could find of the psychological tendencies encouraged in ourselves by their impact, when accepted as a constructive gift of life, is as follows:

Ray 1:   The tendency, innate and ineradicable, to blend and synthesize.
Ray 2:   The quality of the hidden vision.
Ray 3:   The instinct to formulate a plan.
Ray 4:   The urge to creative life, through the divine faculty of imagination.
Ray 5:   The factor of analysis.
Ray 6:   The quality, innate in man, to idealize.
Ray 7:   The interplay of the great dualities.

These phrases are used as sub-headings in Chapter 1 under the 'rules for inducing soul-control' and for assisting the spiritual aspect of the ray energies to manifest. — *A Treatise on the Seven Rays,* Vol. II.

Appendix C

The chart overleaf offers a diagrammatical explanation of the constitution of a human being in relation to the various levels of manifestation in our plane of existence. However, as Ian Gordon-Brown never tires of saying to his transpersonal psychology workshop participants, 'The map is not the country'.

The second, more detailed, chart on the next page, illustrates how the link between the human personality and the triune spiritual nature can be made via the soul or unfolding causal nature. This unfoldment involves the building of a relationship in consciousness, an 'antahkarana' or inner instrument across the seeming void (the upper part of Plane 5 representing the mental/manasic nature) between the higher/inner and the lower/outer mind. This chart also demonstrates the lines of least resistance for energy flow between the various chakras or subtle energy centres, situated within each level of the substance ('the three worlds of human evolution') used by the human being within the personality. This indicates how the unfoldment of our interior nature within manifestation can effect changes in its personality or mask nature.

The third chart in this series of four shows in more detailed enlargement, the so-called causal lotus. A.A.B. pictures it as a flower of energy or flame which blossoms over the centuries of incarnated human living. It is here drawn with a ninefold structure of petals (three of knowledge, three of love and three of sacrifice) which must each unfold as the human soul nature matures; until the work is done, the bridge in light is built, the flower passes away and the spiritual triadic principle is revealed unimpeded.

The 'area of promise' wherein the divine thought is projected, directed and held true to the originating impulse of the planetary Logos is to be found on cosmic levels and remains their unchangeably. It is that which holds Sanat Kumara, in His Council Chamber at Shamballa, standing steadfastly by all those lives which are undergoing redemption and by all those who are the agents of the redemptive process until 'the last weary pilgrim has found his way home'. These agents are the sons of men who will — each and all — demonstrate eventually 'within the courts of Heaven' and at the place of initiation, the nature of their high calling; they will prove to all who can grasp the significance of the demonstration that they have only 'become again in full expression what they have always been'. Now the removal of the veils of matter permits the inner glory to shine forth and — the redemptive work now being finished — 'they can walk with glory in creative undertakings'.

Discipleship in the New Age, Vol. II, page 387.

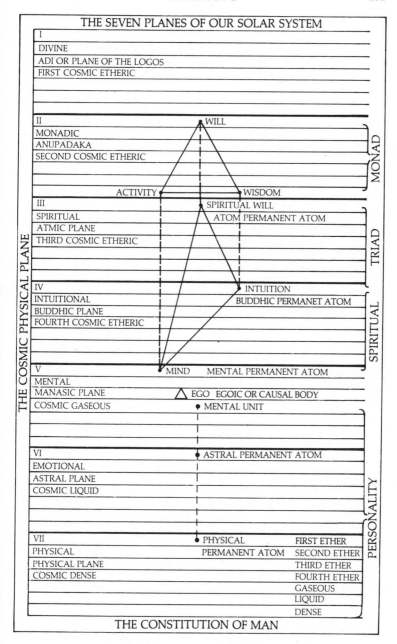

THE SEVEN PLANES OF OUR SOLAR SYSTEM

Letters on Occult Meditation.

Cosmic Physical Plane

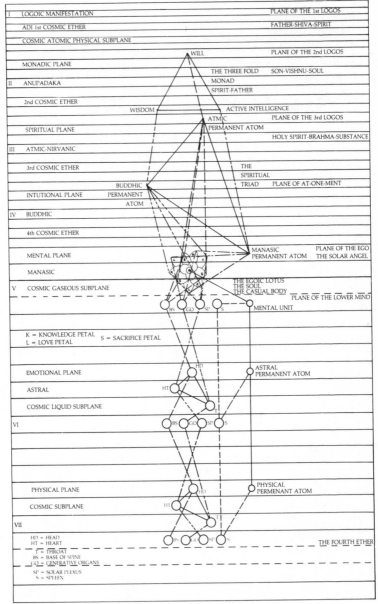

A Treatise on Cosmic Fire, page 817.

The Cosmic Gaseous Subplane

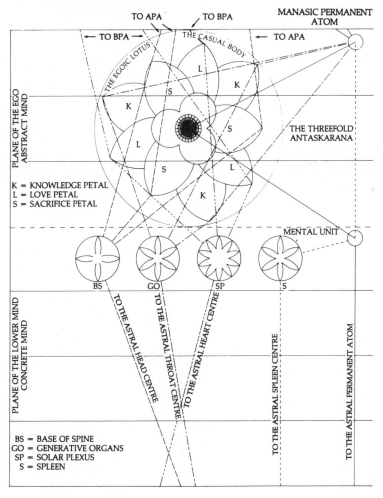

A Treatise on Cosmic Fire, page 823.

Reflection of the Spiritual Triad in the Personality

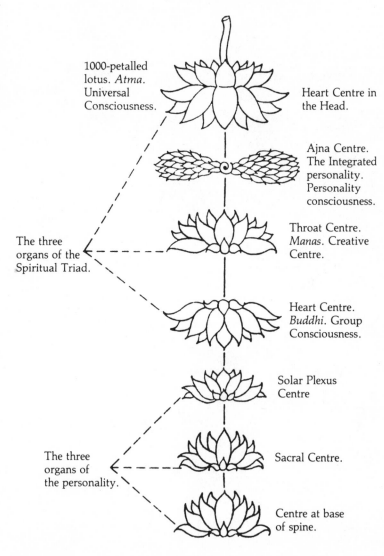

1000-petalled lotus. *Atma.* Universal Consciousness.

Heart Centre in the Head.

Ajna Centre. The Integrated personality. Personality consciousness.

The three organs of the Spiritual Triad.

Throat Centre. *Manas.* Creative Centre.

Heart Centre. *Buddhi.* Group Consciousness.

Solar Plexus Centre

The three organs of the personality.

Sacral Centre.

Centre at base of spine.

The reflection of the Spiritual Triad in the personality is complete when the Ajna Centre is entirely under the control of the soul. There is no attempt in this diagram to picture the correct number of petals in each lotus.

A Treatise on the Seven Rays, Vol. IV, Esoteric Healing.

Appendix D

An example of the kind of reflective outline used for making a creative approach to the hierarchical Lodge at the time of the full moon:

The time of the full moon is a period when spiritual energies are uniquely available, and facilitate a closer rapport between humanity and the Hierarchy. Each month the inflowing energies carry the specific qualities of the constellation influencing the particular month; these energies playing sequentially upon humanity, establish the 'divine attributes' in the consciousness of men. Aspirants seek to channel the spiritual inflow into the minds and hearts of men, and thus strengthen the link between the human kingdom and the Kingdom of God.

Entrance upon the Path of Approach is possible for individuals, for groups, and for humanity as a whole unit. Energies not usually or normally contacted, can be touched, grasped and utilized at the time of these Approaches, provided that they are contacted in group formation. Thus the individual, the group and humanity, are enriched and vitalized.

The Sixfold progression of Divine Love

1. Stand, by an act of the creative imagination, within that centre of consciousness which is the New Group of World Servers, united with all those who approach the Hierarchy in meditation at the period of the full moon. Use the mantram of the Group, as an act of alignment.

   Raise consciousness to the Hierarchy of Masters; to the Christ, the Master of Masters; and to Shamballa, where the will of God is known.

   Stand receptive as a group to the extra-planetary energies available.

2. Visualize a Path of Light stretching between humanity and

the Hierarchy to the feet of the Christ. Visualize the Christ
as the centre of fusion for the aspiration of humanity and
the down-pouring Love of God.
3. Working within the 'six-fold progression of divine love',
    a) visualize the Will-to-Good as 'essential love' pouring from
    b) Shamballa into the Hierarchy, the planetary heart centre.
    c) Bring the flow of Love to a point of focus within the
        Christ, the Heart of Love within the Hierarchy. Stand
        as if before the Christ, and dedicate the group with whom
        you are in contact to world service in His name:

        In the centre of all Love I stand; from that centre I, the Soul,
        will outward move; from that centre I, the one who serves,
        will work. May the Love of the Divine Self be shed abroad
        in my heart, through my group and throughout the world.

    d) Moving with the stream of Love from the Christ to the
        New Group of world servers, embodying the light and
        love needed in the world today, we take our stand within
        the heart and soul of this mediating group. At this point
        of fusion between humanity and Hierarchy we meditate
        on an appropriate seed thought.

        Astrological keynotes:
        Aries —   I come forth and from the plane of mind,
                         I rule.
        Taurus —   I see, and when the eye is opened, all is
                         illumined.
        Gemini —   I recognize my other self, and in the
                         waning of that self I grow and glow.
        Cancer —   I build a lighted house and therein dwell.
        Leo —   I am That and That I am.
        Virgo —   I am the Mother and the Child; I God,
                         I matter am.
        Libra —   I choose the way that leads between the
                         two great lines of force.
        Scorpio —   Warrior I am, and from the battle I
                         emerge triumphant.
        Sagittarius — I see the goal. I reach the goal and see
                         another.
        Capricorn —   Lost am I in light supernal, yet on that
                         light I turn my back.

Aquarius —   Water of life am I, poured forth for
thirsty men.

Pisces —   I leave the Father's Home and turning
back, I save.

e) We transmit the tide of Love into the men and women
of goodwill everywhere in the world, visualizing the
radiation of love creating lines of lighted relationship
between men and nations.

f) Consider 'a focal point through which the Lord of Love
can work on Earth', knowing that through such focal
points, Light, Love and Power make contact with the
minds, the hearts and the little wills of men, weaving all
separated units of life together in consciousness, and
closing 'the door where evil dwells'.

4. Radiate the energy released:

The Great Invocation

From the point of light within the Mind of God
Let Light stream forth into the minds of men.
Let Light descend on Earth.

From the point of Love within the Heart of God
Let Love stream forth into the hearts of men.
May Christ return to Earth.

From the centre where the Will of God is known
Let purpose guide the little wills of men —
The purpose which the Masters know and serve.

From the centre which we call the race of men
Let the Plan of Love and Light work out.
And may it seal the door where evil dwells.

Let Light and Love and Power restore the Plan on Earth.

Sound the sacred word: OM.

List of Groups and Organizations

The Lucis Trust, and The Lucis Press/Publishing Co. (Agency for The Arcane School, World Goodwill and Triangles.)
1. 866 United Nations Plaza, Suite 566-7, New York. N.Y.10017-1888, U.S.A.
2. 3 Whitehall Court, Suite 54, London SW1A 2EF, U.K.
3. 1 Rue de Varembé (3e), Case Postale 31, 1211 Geneva 20, Switzerland.

School for Esoteric Studies, Suite 1903, 40 East 49th. St., New York, N.Y.10017, U.S.A.

Arcana Workshops, P.O. Box 506, Manhattan Beach, Ca. 90266-0506, U.S.A.

Meditation Groups, Inc., Meditation Mount, P.O. Box 566, Ojai, Ca. 93023, U.S.A.

Meditation Group for the New Age, Sundial House, Nevill Park, Tunbridge Wells, Kent, U.K.

Planetary Citizens, 777 United Nations Plaza, New York, N.Y.10017, U.S.A.

The Centre for Trans-Personal Psychology, The Studio, 8 Elsworthy Terrace, London N.W.3, U.K.

Astrologisch-Psychologisches Institut, Postfach 87, CH-8134 Adliswil, Rütistr. 5, Switzerland.

I should emphasize that this short list mentions only the service agency started by Alice and Foster Bailey and a few of the activities initiated by others who, at one time or another, were publicly associated with the headquarter's staff of the Lucis Trust.

Confidentiality does not allow discussion of the many projects started by those who may have been students of the school, for long or short periods; nor does inclusion on this list necessarily mean that the activities of the groups mentioned here proceed entirely on the lines discussed by A.A.B. in her written works. One can only say that the motive of these groups is service and that they use practices which the experience of the individuals concerned in running them have found to be useful and helpful.

References

Introduction:
1. Frances Yates, *The Rosicrucian Enlightenment* and *Giordano Bruno*, (Routledge and Kegan Paul, 1972 and 1964).
2. Alice A. Bailey, *Disciplineship in the New Age Vol I*, (Lucis Press, 1944), p.45.
3. Vera Stanley Alder, *The Finding of the Third Eye*, (Rider, 1939).
4. Alice A. Bailey, *The Unfinished Autobiography*, (Lucis Press, 1951).

Chapter 1
1. Frances Yates, *The Rosicrucian Enlightenment*, (Routledge and Kegan Paul, 1972).
2. R. Trowbridge, *Cagliostro*.
3. Alice A. Bailey, *The Unfinished Autobiography*, (Lucis Press, 1951), p.246.
   Alice A. Bailey, *Discipleship in the New Age, Vol II*, (Lucis Press, 1955), p.429.
4. Aldous Huxley, *The Island*, (Chatto & Windus, 1962).
5. *The Letters of Helena Roerich* and *Hierarchy*, (Agni Yoga, 1931).
6. Alice A. Bailey, *The Unfinished Autobiography*, (Lucis Press, 1951), p.144.
7. *Ibid.*, p.34.
8. Alice A. Bailey, *Initiation, Human and Solar*, (Lucis Press, 1922), p.50.
   Alice A. Bailey, *A Treatise on the Seven Rays, Vol. V*, (Lucis Press, 1960).
9. Alice A. Bailey, *The Unfinished Autobiography*, (Lucis Press, 1951), pp.35-6.
10. *Ibid.*, p.158.
11. *Ibid.*, p.162.
12. Gregory Tillett, *The Elder Brother: Charles Webster Leadbeater*, (Routledge and Kegan Paul, 1982), p.279.

13. Alice A. Bailey, *A Treatise on the Seven Rays, Vol V.*, (Lucis Press, 1960), p.279.
14. *The Beacon* magazine, June 1925.
15. Alice A. Bailey, *The Unfinished Autobiography*, (Lucis Press, 1951), p.164.
16. Alice A. Bailey, *A Treatise on Cosmic Fire*, (Lucis Press, 1925), p.xv.
17. Jane Roberts, *The Individual and the Nature of Mass Events*, (Prentice Hall, 1981).
18. Ruth White and Mary Swainson, *The Healing Spectrum*, (Neville Spearman, 1979).
19. Account by Judith Skutch.
20. Alice A. Bailey, *Discipleship in the New Age*, Vol II, (Lucis Press, 1955), pp.10-11.
21. C. G. Jung (A. Jaffé ed.), *Memories, Dreams, Reflections*, (Collins, 1967).
22. B.B.C. Television Film on Prof. C. G. Jung. Commentary by Sir Laurens van der Post.
23. Alice A. Bailey, *The Unfinished Autobiography*, (Lucis Press, 1951), p.165.
24. Tour guide lecture.
25. Alice A. Bailey, *The Externalisation of the Hierarchy*, (Lucis Press, 1957), p.568.
26. *Ibid.*, p.522.
27. James Hilton, *The Lost Horizon*, (Macmillan, 1962).
28. Alice A. Bailey, *Discipleship in the New Age*, Vol II, (Lucis Press, 1955), p.531.
29. Lecture by H. E. The Tai Situ Pa, 1981.
30. Alice A. Bailey, *The Unfinished Autobiography*, (Lucis Press, 1951), p.297.
31. Alice A. Bailey, *The Light of the Soul*, (Lucis Press, 1927), p.vii.
32. Charles Johnston, *The Yoga Sutras of Pantanjali*, (Watkins).
33. Alice A. Bailey, *The Light of the Soul*, (Lucis Press, 1927), pp.313-5.
34. Alice A. Bailey, *A Treatise on White Magic*, (Lucis Press, 1934), pp.638-9.
35. Sidney Rose-Neil, *Acupuncture and the Life Energies*, (British Acupuncture Association, 1979), p.79.
36. Alice A. Bailey, *The Unfinished Autobiography*, (Lucis Press, 1951), pp.112-6.
37. *ibid.*, p.72.
38. *ibid.*, p.82.
39. *ibid.*, p.280, 300.
40. *ibid.*, Introduction, p.I.
41. Alice A. Bailey, Discipleship in the New Age, Vol. I, (Lucis Press, 1944), p.238, pp.567-8.

42. Alice A. Bailey, *The Externalisation of the Hierarchy*, (Lucis Press, 1957), pp.12-13.
43. Alice A. Bailey, *Discipleship in the New Age*, Vol. II, (Lucis Press, 1955), p.85.
44. Morton Schatzman, *The Story of Ruth*, (Duckworth, 1982).
45. A. P. Sinnett, *The Mahatma Letters to A. P. Sinnett*, (Theosophical Publishing House, 1923), p.107.
Alice A. Bailey, *A Treatise on the Seven Rays*, Vol. V, (Lucis Press, 1060), p.705.
46. *ibid.*, p.190.
47. Alice A. Bailey, *Initiation, Human and Solar*, (Lucis press, 1922), p.58.
48. E. Cooper-Oakley, *The Comte St Germain*, (Theosophical Society). Manly Palmer Hall, *The Most Holy Trinosophia of the Comte de St Germain*, (Philosophers Press, 1949).
49. Alice A. Bailey, *Initiation, Human and Solar*, (Lucis Press, 1922), p.60.
50. Jean Overton Fuller, *Sir Francis Bacon*, (East-West, 1981).
51. Alice A. Bailey, *Initiation, Human and Solar*, (Lucis Press, 1922), p.58.
52. *ibid.*
53. Alice A. Bailey, *The Unfinished Autobiography*, (Lucis Press, 1951), p.190.
54. Alice A. Bailey, *A Treatise on the Seven Rays*, Vol. IV, (Lucis Press, 1953), p.360.
55. Alice A. Bailey, *Telepathy and the Etheric Vehicle*, (Lucis Press, 1950), p.83.
56. *ibid.*, p.4.
57. Alice A. Bailey, *A Treatise on the Seven Rays*, Vol. V, (Lucis Press, 1960), p.119.
58. Alice A. Bailey, *Discipleship in the New Age*, Vol. II, (Lucis Press, 1955), p.103.
59. Gary Zukav, *The Dancing Wu Li Masters*, (Rider, 1979), p.73.
60. Alice A. Bailey, *Telepathy and the Etheric Vehicle*, (Lucis Press, 1950), p.85.
61. Alice A. Bailey, *The Unfinished Autobiography*, (Lucis Press, 1949), pp.207-8.
62. H. S. Burr, *Blueprint for Immortality*, (Neville Spearman, 1972).
63. Alice A. Bailey, *Discipleship in the New Age*, Vol. I, (Lucis Press, 1944), p.24.
64. Talbot Mundy, *OM: Secret of Ahbor Valley*, (Point Loma, 1924).
65. Gary Zukav, *The Dancing Wu Li Masters*, (Rider, 1979), p.34.
66. Alice A. Bailey, *A Treatise on the Seven Rays*, Vol. V, (Lucis Press, 1960), pp.368-9.

67. Alice A. Bailey, *Initiation, Human and Solar*, (Lucis Press, 1922), p.29.
68. Joseph Campbell, *The Masks of God*, (Souvenir Press 1960-74). Workshop on Myth with Joan Swallow.
69. Alice A. Bailey, *Initiation, Human and Solar*, (Lucis Press, 1922), pp.59-60.
70. The Collected Plays of J. M. Barrie.
71. Emily Lutyens, *Candles in the Sun*.
72. Marjorie Pentland, *Lord Pentland, A Memoir* (Methuen 1928).
73. Alice A. Bailey, *Discipleship in the New Age*, Vol. I, (Lucis Press, 1944), p.42.

Chapter 2:
1. Alice A. Bailey, *The Unfinished Autobiography*, (Lucis Press, 1951), p.138.
2. *ibid.*, p.154.
3. *ibid.*, p.190-1.
4. *ibid.*, p.193.
5. *ibid.*, p.300, also *Discipleship in the New Age*, Vol. II, (1955), pp.83-4, 87, 101.
6. Alice A. Bailey, *The Unfinished Autobiography*, (Lucis Press, 1951), p.190.
7. *ibid.*, p.199.
8. *ibid.*, p.25.
9. *ibid.*, p.25.
10. *ibid.*, p.17.
11. *ibid.*, p.31.
12. *A Treatise on White Magic*, (1934), p.602.
13. Arcane School full-moon meditation paper; also Alice A. Bailey, *Discipleship in the New Age*, Vol. II, p.113., and *Letters on Occult Meditation*, (Lucis Press, 1955 and 1922).
14. Alice A. Bailey, *Education in the New Age*, (Lucis Press), p.32.
15. Alice A. Bailey, *A Treatise on the Seven Rays*, Vol. V, (Lucis Press, 1960), p.450. and
    Alice A. Bailey, *Discipleship in the New Age*, Vol. II, (Lucis Press, 1955), p.193.
16. Alice A. Bailey, *The Externalisation of the Hierarchy*, (Lucis Press, 1957), p.606, and
    A Treatise on the Seven Rays, Vol. V, (1960), pp.290, 524 and 722.
17. *ibid.*, pp.441-530; also Alice A. Bailey, *The Reappearance of Christ*, p.28.
18. Alice A. Bailey, *A Treatise on Cosmic Fire*, (Lucis Press, 1925), p.137, also
    Discipleship in the New Age, Vol. II, (1955), p.194.

19. Eastern term for emotional-mental substance forming part of human personality.
20. Robert Assagioli M.D., *Psychosynthesis: A Manual of Principles and Techniques*, (Turnstone Press, 1965).
21. World Goodwill paper on invocation.
22. *Shamanism: Archaic Techniques of Ecstasy*, Mircea Eliade, (Pantheon, 1964), p.83.
23. *St John of the Cross*, Part II, Book II, Chap 20.
24. *Hebrews* 11.1.
25. H. P. Blavatsky, *Thoughts on the Gita*, (Theosophical Publishing House).
    Alice A. Bailey, *Initiation, Human and Solar*, (Lucis Press, 1922), p.74.
26. Viz., The Norns which appear in Wagner's music drama *The Ring of the Nibelungen*.
27. *Ecclesiastes* 12.6.
28. Carrington and Muldoon, *The Projection of the Astral Body*, (Rider, 1929).
    Stavely Bulford, *Man's Unknown Journey*.
29. Alice A. Bailey, *Telepathy and the Etheric Vehicle*, (Lucis Press, 1950), p.53.
30. Arcane school meditation paper for the full-moon approach. See also *Discipleship in the New Age*, Vol. II, (Lucis Press, 1955), pp.55-59.
31. *ibid.*, p.15.
32. Alice A. Bailey, *The Destiny of the Nations*, (Lucis Press, 1949), p.151.
33. Letter to students and workers of the Arcane School.
34. Alice A. Bailey, *The Unfinished Autobiography*, (Lucis Press, 1951), p.228.
35. *ibid.*, p.220.
36. *ibid.*, p.230.
37. Letter to students and workers of the Arcane School.
38. *ibid.*
39. Alice A. Bailey, *Discipleship in the New Age*, Vol. II, (Lucis Press, 1955), p.133.
    Also *Telepathy and the Etheric Vehicle*, (1950), p.163.
    Also *A Treatise on the Seven Rays*, Vol. V, (1960), p.253.
40. Alice A. Bailey, *Discipleship in the New Age*, Vol. II, (Lucis Press, 1955), p.62.
41. Jonathan Fryer, *Isherwood: A Biography of Christopher Isherwood*, (New English Library, 1977).
42. Ven. Chogyam Trungpa, *The Myth of Freedom*, (Shambala, 1976), pp.104-5.

43. Letter to students and workers of the Arcane School.

Chapter 3:
1. Letter to students and workers of the Arcane School, p.19.
2. *ibid.*, p.22.
3. Alice A. Bailey, *Discipleship in the New Age*, Vol. I, (Lucis Press, 1944), p.272.
4. Alice A. Bailey, *Initiation, Human and Solar*, (Lucis Press, 1922), p.224.
5. Alice A. Bailey, *A Treatise on the Seven Rays*, Vol. V, (Lucis Press, 1960), p.556.
6. Conversation with Leonard Elmhirst.
7. Alice A. Bailey, *The Unfinished Autobiography*, (Lucis Press, 1951), p.27.
8. Alice A. Bailey, *Discipleship in the New Age*, Vol. II, (Lucis Press, 1955), p.390.
9. Alice A. Bailey, *The Unfinished Autobiography*, (Lucis Press, 1951), p.294.
10. *ibid.*, pp.55, 112.
11. Infinite Way closed classwork given by Joel S. Goldsmith.
12. Alice A. Bailey, *A Treatise on the Seven Rays*, Vol. III, (Esoteric Astrology), (Lucis Press, 1951), p.101.
13. Conversation with William Blewett.
14. *Exodus* 5.7.
15. Alice A. Bailey, *The Unfinished Autobiography*, (Lucis Press, 1951), pp.103, 128.
16. 2 *Corinthians* 6.10.
17. Alice A. Bailey, *Discipleship in the New Age*, Vol. I., (Lucis Press, 1944), pp.271-2.
18. *ibid.*, vol.1, pp.272-3.
19. *ibid.*, vol.1, pp.231, 228.
20. Alice A. Bailey, *A Treatise on the Seven Rays*, Vol. II, (Lucis Press 1942), p.736.
21. Letter to students and workers of the Arcane School, p.21.
22. Alice A. Bailey, *The Externalisation of the Hierarchy*, (Lucis Press, 1957), p.664.
23. *ibid.*, p.664.
24. *ibid.*, p.664.
25. Alice A. Bailey, *The Externalisation of the Hierarchy*, (Lucis Press, 1957), p.665.
26. *ibid.*, p.666.
27. *ibid.*, p.668.
28. Alice A. Bailey, *A Treatise on Cosmic Fire*, (Lucis Press, 1925), p.755.

29. Alice A. Bailey, *Discipleship in the New Age*, Vol. I, (Lucis Press, 1955), pp.673-773.
30. Helena Roerich (Agri Yoga Society, Inc.).
31. Alice A. Bailey, *Discipleship in the New Age*, Vol. II, (Lucis Press, 1955), p.103.
32. Edwin Bernbaum, *The Way to Shambhala*, (Anchor Books, 1980), p.229.
33. Alice A. Bailey, *Letters on Occult Meditation*, (Lucis Press, 1922), p.142.
34. Alice A. Bailey, *Discipleship in the New Age*, Vol. I, (Lucis Press, 1944), p.270.
35. Letter to students and workers of the Arcane School.
36. Alice A. Bailey, *The Externalisation of the Hierarchy*, (Lucis Press, 1957), p.142.

Chapter 4:
 1. Alice A. Bailey, *The Externalisation of the Hierarchy*, (Lucis Press, 1957), p.169.
 2. Alice A. Bailey, *The Unfinished Autobiography*, (Lucis Press, 1951), p.236.
 3. *A Treatise on the Seven Rays*, Vol. IV, (Esoteric Healing), (Lucis press, 1953), p.433. Also *Discipleship in the New Age*, Vol. I, (1944), p.101.
 4. Alice A. Bailey, *A Treatise on the Seven Rays*, Vol. IV, (Lucis Press, 1953), p.387.
 5. *ibid.*, pp437-447., also *A Treatise on White Magic*, (1934), p.494.
 6. Alice A. Bailey, *A Treatise on the Seven Rays*, Vol. IV, (Lucis Press, 1953) — see Index.
    Alice A. Bailey, *A Treatise on Cosmic Fire*, (Lucis Press, 1925), pp.128-133.
 7. Conversation between the Ven. Sogyal Rinpoche and myself.
 8. Alice A. Bailey, *A Treatise on the Seven Rays*, Vol. IV, (Lucis Press, 1953), p.457.
 9. Alice A. Bailey, *The Externalisation of the Hierarchy*, (Lucis Press, 1957), p.410.
10. Alice A. Bailey, *Discipleship in the New Age*, Vol. II, (Lucis Press, 1955), p.101.
11. Alice A. Bailey, *The Reappearance of Christ*, (Lucis Press, 1948), p.115.
12. Alice A. Bailey, *The Externalisation of the Hierarchy*, (Lucis Press, 1957), p.116/7.
13. Charles Kingsley, *The Water Babies*, (Gollancz, 1961).
14. *Discipleship in the New Age*, Vol. II, (Lucis Press, 1955), p.541.
15. Nancy Magor and M. J. Eastcott, *The Phenomena of Death* and

Pain and its Transforming Power, (Sundial House Publications).
16. Alice A. Bailey, A Treatise on the Seven Rays, Vol. II, (Lucis Press, 1942), p.217.
17. Alice A. Bailey, The Externalisation of the Hierarchy, (Lucis Press, 1957), p.669.
18. Alice A. Bailey, Discipleship in the New Age, Vol. I, (Lucis Press, 1944), pp.105-670:
    and Vol. II, (1955), pp.443-764.
19. Alice A. Bailey, Discipleship in the New Age, Vol. I, (Lucis Press, 1944), p.ix.
20. ibid., Vol. II, p.103.
21. ibid., Vol. I, pp.xii-xiii.
22. ibid., Vol. II, p.94.
23. ibid., Vol. II, p.104.
24. ibid., Vol. II, p.104, (Part 2).
25. ibid., Vol. II, p.515.
26. ibid., Vol. I, p.xiii.
27. ibid., Vol. II, p.90.
28. Alice A. Bailey, A Treatise on the Seven Rays, Vol. II, (Lucis Press, 1942), p186.
29. Alice A. Bailey, Discipleship in the New Age, Vol. II, (Lucus Press, 1955) pp.35-42.
30. ibid., Vol. I, p.43, 54.
31. ibid., Vol. I, p.42.
32. Alice A. Bailey, Discipleship in the New Age, Vol. I, (Lucis Press, 1944), pp. 36-40.
33. Alice A. Bailey, The Externalisation of the Hierarchy, (Lucis Press, 1957), pp.36-7 & 64.
34. Alice A. Bailey, Telepathy and the Etheric Vehicle, (Lucis Press, 1950), p.135.
    Alice A. Bailey, A Treatise on the Seven Rays, Vol. V, (Lucis Press, 1960), p.456.
35. Alice A. Bailey, A Treatise on Cosmic Fire, (Lucis Press, 1925), p.818.
36. Alice A. Bailey, A Treatise on the Seven Rays, Vol. V, (Lucis Press, 1960), pp.456 and 661-763.
37. Alice A. Bailey, A Treatise on the Seven Rays, Vol. II, (Lucis Press, 1942), p.197.
38. William Shakespeare, Macbeth Act 1. sc. iii.
39. The Ninth Configuration.
40. Edwin Bernbaum, The Way to Shambhala, (Anchor Books, 1980), p.145, also Rebirth — the Tibetan Game of Liberation, p.59.
41. A talk by Warren Kenton.
42. J. G. Bennett, Making a New World, (Turnstone Press, 1973), p.293.

43. John Anthony West, *Serpent in the Sky*, (Wildwood House, 1979), p.68.
44. Alice A. Bailey, *The Externalisation of the Hierarchy*, (Lucis Press, 1957), p.47.
45. *The Oxford Pocket Dictionary*.
46. John Anthony West, *Serpent in the Sky*, (Wildwood House, 1979), p.67.
47. *Infinity*, Vol. II, (Agni Yoga Society, 1930), p.39.
48. Alice A. Bailey, *A Treatise on the Seven Rays*, Vol. IV, (Lucis Press, 1953), p.362.
49. Information on this theme is also to be found in H. P. Blavatsky's, *The Secret Doctrine*, Vol. II, (3-volume edition), (Theosophical Publishing House, 1888), pp.183, 185, 274, 298, 717.
50. Alice A. Bailey, *A Treatise on the Seven Rays*, Vol. III, (Esoteric Astrology), (Lucis Press, 1951), p.264.
51. *ibid.*, p.3 and Appendix p.635.
52. Alice A. Bailey, *A Treatise on White Magic*, (Lucis Press, 1934), p.520.
53. Edwin Bernbaum, *The Way to Shambhala*, (Anchor Books, 1980).
54. Alice A. Bailey, *Discipleship in the New Age*, Vol. II, (1955), pp.527-8.
55. *ibid.*, pp.519-20.
56. Edwin Bernbaum, *The Way to Shambhala*, (Anchor Books, 1980), p.10.
57. Alice A. Bailey, *A Treatise on White Magic*, (Lucis Press, 1934), p.378.
58. John R. Sinclair, *The Mystical Ladder*, (S.A.G.B., 1968), p.59.
59. Alice A. Bailey, *A Treatise on the Seven Rays*, Vol. V, (Lucis Press, 1960), p.143.
60. Alice A. Bailey, *A Treatise on White Magic*, (Lucis Press, 1934), p.403.
61. Alice A. Bailey, *The Unfinished Autobiography*, (Lucis Press, 1951), p.192.
62. Edwin Bernbaum, *The Way to Shambhala*, (Anchor Books, 1980), p.105.
63. Alice A. Bailey, *The Externalisation of the Hierarchy*, (Lucis Press, 1957), p.568.
64. Alice A. Bailey, *A Treatise on the Seven Rays*, Vol. V, (Lucis Press, 1957), p.380.
65. Alice A. Bailey, *The Externalisation of the Hierarchy*, (Lucis Press, 1957), pp.505, 577.
66. Alice A. Bailey, *A Treatise on the Seven Rays*, Vol. V, (Lucis Press, 1960), pp.139-142.
67. *ibid.*, Vol. III, p.581.

68. Alice A. Bailey, *Discipleship in the New Age*, Vol. II, (Lucis Press, 1955), p.515.
69. Alice A. Bailey, *The Externalisation of the Hierarchy*, (Lucis Press, 1957), pp.71/2.
70. T. S. Eliot, *Four Quartets*, 'Little Gidding' (Faber, 1944).
71. Alice A. Bailey, *Telepathy and the Etheric Vehicle*, (Lucis Press, 1950), p.197.

Chapter 5:
 1. The Title: Ajna Centre of the World from *A Treatise on the Seven Rays*, Vol. V, (1960), p.368.
 2. Alice A. Bailey, *A Treatise on White Magic*, (Lucis Press, 1934), p.580.
 3. Alice A. Bailey, *A Treatise on the Seven Rays*, Vol. V, (Lucis Press, 1960), p.107.
 4. Alice A. Bailey, *A Treatise on Cosmic Fire*, (Lucis Press, 1925), pp.280-1.
 5. Alice A. Bailey, *Discipleship in the New Age*, Vol. I, (Lucis Press, 1944), p.256.
 6. *ibid.*, Vol. II, pp.451-3, Vol. I, pp.213 and 246.
 7. Alice A. Bailey, *Discipleship in the New Age*, Vol. II, (Lucis Press, 1955), pp.15, 26-7, 51-57.
 8. Robert K. G. Temple, *The Sirius Mystery*, (St Martins Press, 1976), p.97.
 9. Alice A. Bailey, *Disciplineship in the New Age*, Vol. I, (Lucis Press, 1944), p.165.
10. World Goodwill pamphlet on the New Group of World Servers; *A Treatise on the Seven Rays*, Vol. II, (1942), pp.724-51.
11. World Goodwill pamphlet on the New Group of World Servers.
12. *ibid.*
13. Alice A. Bailey, *A Treatise on White Magic*, (Lucis Press, 1934), pp.428-31.
14. *ibid.*
15. Alice A. Bailey, *A Treatise on the Seven Rays*, Vol. II, (Lucis Press, 1942), p.197.
16. Alice A. Bailey, *A Treatise on White Magic*, (Lucis Press, 1934), p.430.
17. *ibid.*, pp.102-3, 317.
18. *A Course in Miracles*, Vol. II, Workbook for Students: Lesson 66, p.109, (Foundation for Inner Peace, 1975).
19. Helena Roerich, *Heart*, (Agni Yoga Publications, 1932), p.60.
20. Alice A. Bailey, *A Treatise on White Magic*, (Lucis Press, 1934), p.102.
21. *ibid.*, p.430.

22. *ibid.*, p.425.
23. Teilhard de Chardin, *Building the Earth*, (Editions du Seuil, 1958).
24. Observer Colour Magazine.
25. Scientific and Medical Network Newsletter No. 1.
26. 27 February 1977.
27. Marilyn Ferguson, *The Aquarian Conspiracy*, (Granada, 1982).
28. Ursula LeGuin, *The Left Hand of Darkness*, (Macdonald & Co.).
29. Alexander Solzhenitsyn, *One Word of Truth*, (The Bodley Head, 1970).
30. *ibid.*, p.30.
31. The Principle of Universal Responsibility. His Holiness the Dalai Lama XIV, (Library of Tibetan Works and Archives, 1976).
32. (Agni Yoga Press).
33. Foster Bailey, *The Meaning of Masonry*, (Lucis Press, 1957), p.78.
34. *Observer.*
35. Alice A. Bailey, *A Treatise on White Magic*, (Lucis Press, 1934), p.403.
36. Foster Bailey, *The Meaning of Masonry*, (Lucis Press, 1957), pp.79-80.
37. *Matthew* 4.19.
38. Alice A. Bailey, *A Treatise on the Seven Rays*, Vol. V, (Lucis Press, 1960), p.375.
39. Alice A. Bailey, *A Treatise on the Seven Rays*, Vol. V, (Lucis Press, 1960), p.376.
40. *ibid.*, p.374.
41. *John* 14.2.
42. Alice A. Bailey, *The Externalisation of the Hierarchy*, (Lucis Press, 1957), p.529.
43. Kahlil Gibran, *The Prophet*, (Heineman, 1926).
44. Robert K. G. Temple, *The Sirius Mystery*, (St Martins Press, 1976), p.72, footnote.
45. Alice A. Bailey, *A Treatise on the Seven Rays*, Vol. V, (Lucis Press, 1960), pp.167-70.
46. *ibid.*, pp.172-3.
47. Alice A. Bailey, *A Treatise on the Seven Rays*, Vol. III, (Esoteric Astrology), (Lucis Press, 1951), p.428.
48. Alice A. Bailey, *A Treatise on the Seven Rays*, Vol. V, (Lucis Press, 1960), pp.380-1.
49. Alice A. Bailey, *A Treatise on White Magic*, (Lucis Press, 1934), p.360.
50. Alice A. Bailey, *A Treatise on the Seven Rays*, Vol. III, (Esoteric Astrology), (Lucis Press, 1951), p.455.
51. *ibid.*, p.428.
52. *ibid.*, p.426.

53. Alice A. Bailey, *The Destiny of Nations*, (Lucis Press, 1949), pp.92-104.
54. *ibid.*, p.102.
55. Alice A. Bailey, *A Treatise on White Magic*, (Lucis Press, 1934), p.409.
56. *ibid.*, p.276.
57. Peter Russell, *The Brain Book*, (Routledge and Kegan Paul, 1979).
58. Alice A. Bailey, *A Treatise on White Magic*, (Lucis Press, 1934), p.74.
59. *ibid.*, p.216.
60. Alice A. Bailey, *Discipleship in the New Age*, Vol. II, (Lucis Press, 1955), p.371.
61. Alice A. Bailey, *A Treatise on the Seven Rays*, Vol. IV, (Esoteric Healing), (Lucis Press, 1953), pp.144-189.
62. Alice A. Bailey, *A Treatise on White Magic*, (Lucis Press, 1934), p.592.
63. *ibid.*, p.422.
64. Walter Starcke, *This Double Thread*, (Harper and Row, 1967). Quotation from de Chardin.
65. John J. O'Niell, *Prodigal Genius: The Life of Nikola Tesla*, (Neville Spearman, 1968).
66. *ibid.*, pp.275-6.
67. Carlos Castaneda, *Journey to Ixtlan*, (Penguin, 1973).
68. H. P. Blavatsky, *The Secret Doctrine*, Vol. I, p.77. Alice A. Bailey, *A Treatise on Cosmic Fire*, (Lucis Press, 1925, p.965, footnote.
69. Alice A. Bailey, *A Treatise on the Seven Rays*, Vol. V, (Lucis Press, 1960), p.122/3.
70. Alice A. Bailey, *A Treatise on the Seven Rays*, Vol. II, (Lucis Press, 1942), p.646.
71. Alice A. Bailey, *A Treatise on White Magic*, (Lucis Press, 1934), p.261.

Chapter 6:
1. Alice A. Bailey, *A Treatise on White Magic*, (Lucis Press, 1934), p.314.
2. Alice A. Bailey, *The Externalisation of the Hierarchy*, (Lucis Press, 1957), pp85-6.
3. Alice A. Bailey, *A Treatise on the Seven Rays*, Vol. V, (Lucis Press, 1960), p.368.
4. Gaston Saint-Pierre and Debbie Boater, *The Metamorphic Technique*, (Element Books, 1982), p.49.
5. Alice A. Bailey, *Discipleship in the New Age*, Vol. II, (Lucis Press, 1955), pp.243-439.

6. *ibid.*, p.249.
7. *ibid.*, p.275.
8. *ibid.*, p.273.
9. Alice A. Bailey, *A Treatise on Seven Rays*, Vol. V, (Lucis Press, 1960), pp.3-285.
10. Communicators — *Telepathy and the Etheric Vehicle;*
    Observers   — *Glamour, A World Problem;*
    Healers   — *A Treatise on the Seven Rays*, Vol. IV;
    Educators   — *Education in the New Age;*
    Politics   — *The Destiny of the Nations;*
    Religion   — *The Reappearance of Christ.*
11. Alice A. Bailey, *Initiation, Human and Solar*, (Lucis Press, 1922), p.222.
12. Alice A. Bailey, *The Externalisation of the Hierarchy*, (Lucis Press, 1957), p.541.
13. Alice A. Bailey, *A Treatise on Cosmic Fire*, (Lucis Press, 1925), p.779.
14. H. P. Blavatsky, *The Voice of Silence*, (Theosophical Publishing House, 1889), p.97.
15. Alice A. Bailey, *A Treatise on Cosmic Fire*, (Lucis Press, 1925), pp.1192-4.
16. Alice A. Bailey, *A Treatise on White Magic*, (Lucis Press, 1934), p.429.
17. Alice A. Bailey, *Letters on Occult Meditation*, (Lucis Press, 1922), p.298.
18. *ibid.*, p.300.
19. *ibid.*, p.301. Also, *The Destiny of Nations*, (1949), p.132, and *A Treatise on White Magic*, (1934), p.79.
20. The books of Frances Yates, (Routledge and Kegan Paul). Lincoln, Leigh and Baigent, *The Holy Blood and the Holy Grail*, Section 1, (Jonathan Cape, 1982).
21. Emma Curtis Hopkins, *High Mysticism*, (DeVorss, 1979).
22. Conversation with George Hall.
23. Alice A. Bailey, *A Treatise on the Seven Rays*, Vol. V, (Lucis Press, 1960), p.679.
24. 'Art and Education', *Kalakshetra Journal*, Vol. xvii, No. 4.
25. Infinite Way Closed Class.
26. Alice A. Bailey, *The Externalisation of the Hierarchy*, (Lucis Press, 1957), p.286.
27. Alice A. Bailey, *Discipleship in the New Age*, Vol. I, (Lucis Press, 1944), p.720.
28. Alice A. Bailey, *A Treatise on White Magic*, (Lucis Press, 1934), p.333.
29. Alice A. Bailey, *The Externalisation of the Hierarchy*, (Lucis Press, 1957), pp.491-500.

30. Alice A. Bailey, *A Treatise on Cosmic Fire*, (1925), pp.452, 492-6, 917 and 1066.
31. *ibid.*, p.486.
32. *ibid.*, p.759. Also Alice A. Bailey, *A Treatise on White Magic*, (1934), p.334.
33. Alice A. Bailey, *The Externalisation of the Hierarchy*, (1957), pp.504-8.
34. H. S. Burr, *Blueprint for Immortality*, (Neville Spearman).
35. Shafica Karagulla MD., *Breakthrough to Creativity*, (DeVorss, 1967).
36. Sidney Rose-Neil, *An Acupuncturist Visits China*, (British Acupuncture Association, 1979).
37. East-West Association, (Boston and London).
38. The Institute for Complementary Medicine, London; Health for the New Age Ltd., London; The Natural Health Foundation, London; Search for a Cure for Cancer, U.K.
39. Alice A. Bailey, *A Treatise on White Magic*, (Lucis Press, 1934, p.532.
40. Alice A. Bailey, *A Treatise on Cosmic Fire*, (Lucis Press, 1925), pp.1178, 1241-66.
41. *ibid.*, pp.569-70.
42. *ibid.*, pp.723-4.
43. Conversation with Robert Temple.
44. Alice A. Bailey, *A Treatise on the Seven Rays*, Vol. V, (Lucis Press, 1960), p.251.
45. Alice A. Bailey, *Discipleship in the New Age*, Vol. II, (Lucis Press, 1955), p.101.
46. Alice A. Bailey, *The Unfinished Autobiography*, x-xi, (Lucis Press, 1951).
47. Alice A. Bailey, *A Treatise on White Magic*, (Lucis Press, 1934), p.319.
48. Alice A. Bailey, *A Treatise on Cosmic Fire*, p.748. Also Alice A. Bailey, *The Externalisation of the Hierarchy*, pp.269-74, 304.
49. Alice A. Bailey, *The Reappearance of Christ*, (Lucis Press, 1925, 1957 + 1948).
50. See Index of *A Treatise of Cosmic Fire*, (Lucis Press, 1925).
51. Alice A. Bailey, *The Externalisation of the Hierarchy*, (Lucis Press, 1957).
52. *ibid.*, p.600.
53. Alice A. Bailey, *A Treatise on Cosmic Fire*, (Lucis Press, 1925), p.760.
54. Alice A. Bailey, *A Treatise on the Seven Rays*, Vol. II, (Lucis Press, 1942), p.646.
55. Meeting held at Broadwater Down, Tunbridge Wells on Alice A. Bailey's last visit to UK.

56. Alice A. Bailey, *Discipleship in the New Age*, Vol. II, (Lucis Press, 1955), pp.135-6.
57. Alice A. Bailey, *A Treatise on the Seven Rays*, Vol. II, (Lucis Press, 1942), p.647.
58. Alice A. Bailey, *A Course in Miracles*, Vol. I, Chs 16 and 17. (Foundation for Inner Peace, 1975). Also, Emma Curtis Hopkins, *High Mysticism*, Ch. 3, (DeVorss, 1979).
59. Alice A. Bailey, *The Externalisation of the Hierarchy*, (Lucis Press, 1957), p.139.
60. World Goodwill pamphlet on the New Group of World Servers.
61. Alice A. Bailey, *A Treatise on the Seven Rays*, Vol. II, (Lucis Press, 1942), pp.96-97, 165-66;
    Alice A. Bailey, *Externalisation of the Hierarchy*, (Lucis Press, 1957), pp.118-9.
62. *Luke* 15.20.
63. Alice A. Bailey, *A Treatise on White Magic*, (Lucis Press, 1934), p.314.
64. Commentary Quotation in Old *Discipleship in the New Age*, Vol. II, (1955), pp.314-5.

Index